Serials Management in the Electronic Era: Papers in Honor of Peter Gellatly, Founding Editor of *The Serials Librarian*

Serials Management in the Electronic Era: Papers in Honor of Peter Gellatly, Founding Editor of *The Serials Librarian*

Jim Cole
James W. Williams
Editors

The Haworth Press, Inc.
New York • London

Serials Management in the Electronic Era: Papers in Honor of Peter Gellatly, Founding Editor of The Serials Librarian has also been published as *The Serials Librarian*, Volume 29, Numbers 3/4 1996.

The development, preparation, and publication of this work has been undertaken with great care. However, the publisher, employees, editors, and agents of The Haworth Press and all imprints of The Haworth Press, Inc., including The Haworth Medical Press and Pharmaceutical Products Press, are not responsible for any errors contained herein or for consequences that may ensue from use of materials or information contained in this work. Opinions expressed by the author(s) are not necessarily those of The Haworth Press, Inc.

The Haworth Press, Inc., 10 Alice Street, Binghamton, NY 13904-1580 USA

Library of Congress Cataloging-in-Publication Data

Serials management in the electronic era : papers in honor of Peter Gellatly, founding editor of The serials librarian / Jim Cole, James W. Williams, editors.
    p. cm.
    "Has also been published as The serials librarian, v. 29, no. 3/4, 1996."
    Includes bibliographical references and index.
    ISBN 0-7890-0021-0 (alk. paper)
    1. Serials control systems–United States–Data processing. 2. Serials control systems–United States–Automation. 3. Libraries–United States–Special collections–Electronic journals. I. Cole, Jim E. II. Williams, James W. III. Gellatly, Peter.
Z692.S5S4837 1996
025.3'432'0285–dc20
                                                     96-38911
                                                      CIP

INDEXING & ABSTRACTING

Contributions to this publication are selectively indexed or abstracted in print, electronic, online, or CD-ROM version(s) of the reference tools and information services listed below. This list is current as of the copyright date of this publication. See the end of this section for additional notes.

- *Academic Abstracts/CD-ROM,* EBSCO Publishing, Editorial Department, P.O. Box 590, Ipswich, MA 01938-0590

- *Academic Search: database of 2,000 selected academic serials, updated monthly,* EBSCO Publishing, 83 Pine Street, Peabody, MA 01960

- *Cambridge Scientific Abstracts, Health & Safety Science Abstracts,* Environmental Routenet (accessed via INTERNET), 7200 Wisconsin Avenue, #601, Bethesda, MD 20814

- *Chemical Abstracts,* Chemical Abstracts Service Library, 2540 Olgentangy Road, P.O. Box 3012, Columbus, OH 43210

- *CINAHL (Cumulative Index to Nursing & Allied Health Literature), in print, also on CD-ROM from CD PLUS, EBSCO, and Silver-Platter, and online from CDP Online (formerly BRS), Data-Star, and PaperChase. (Support materials include Subject Heading List, Database Search Guide, and instructional video.)* CINAHL Information Systems, P.O. Box 871, 1509 Wilson Terrace, Glendale, CA 91209-0871

- *CNPIEC Reference Guide: Chinese National Directory of Foreign Periodicals,* P.O. Box 88, Beijing, People's Republic of China

- *Current Awareness Bulletin,* Association for Information Management, Information House, 20-24 Old Street, London, EC1V 9AP, England

- *Current Contents* . . . . . see: *Institute for Scientific Information*

(continued)

- *Hein's Legal Periodical Checklist: Index to Periodical Articles Pertaining to Law,* William S. Hein & Co., Inc., 1285 Main Street, Buffalo, NY 14209

- *IBZ International Bibliography of Periodical Literature,* Zeller Verlag GmbH & Co., P.O.B. 1949, d-49009 Osnabruck, Germany

- *Index to Periodical Articles Related to Law,* University of Texas, 727 East 26th Street, Austin, TX 78705

- *Information Reports & Bibliographies,* Science Associates International, Inc., 6 Hastings Road, Marlboro, NJ 07746-1313

- *Information Science Abstracts,* Plenum Publishing Company, 233 Spring Street, New York, NY 10013-1578

- *Informed Librarian, The,* Infosources Publishing, 140 Norma Road, Teaneck, NJ 07666

- *Institute for Scientific Information,* 3501 Market Street, Philadelphia, Pennsylvania 19104-3302. Coverage in:
  a) Social Science Citation Index (SSCI): print, online, CD-ROM
  b) Research Alert (ISI's current awareness service)
  c) Social SciSearch (magnetic tape, ISI's online database)
  d) Current Contents/Social & Behavioral Sciences (weekly current awareness service)
  e) Clinical Medicine/Life Sciences (CC: CM/LS) (weekly Table of Contents Service)

- *INTERNET ACCESS (& additional networks) Bulletin Board for Libraries ("BUBL"), coverage of information resources on INTERNET, JANET, and other networks.*
  - JANET X.29: UK.AC.BATH.BUBL or 00006012101300
  - TELNET: BUBL.BATH.AC.UK or 138.38.32.45 login 'bubl'
  - Gopher: BUBL.BATH.AC.UK (138.32.32.45). Port 7070
  - World Wide Web: http: / / www.bubl.bath.ac.uk./BUBL/ home.html
  - NISSWAIS: telnetniss.ac.uk (for the NISS gateway)
  The Andersonian Library, Curran Building, 101 St. James Road, Glasgow G4 ONS, Scotland

- *Konyvtari Figyelo-Library Review,* National Szechenyi Library, Centre for Library and Information Science, H-1827 Budapest, Hungary

(continued)

- *Library & Information Science Abstracts (LISA),* Bowker-Saur Limited, Maypole House, Maypole Road, East Grinstead, West Sussex, RH19 1HH, England

- *Library Digest,* Highsmith Press, W5527 Highway 106, P.O. Box 800, Fort Atkinson, WI 53538-0800

- *Library Hi Tech News,* Pierian Press, P.O. Box 1808, Ann Arbor, MI 48106

- *Library Literature,* The H. W. Wilson Company, 950 University Avenue, Bronx, NY 10452

- *MasterFILE: updated database,* EBSCO Publishing, 83 Pine Street, Peabody, MA 01960

- *Newsletter of Library and Information Services,* China Sci-Tech Book Review, Library of Academia Sinica, 8 Kexueyuan Nanlu, Zhongguancun, Beijing 100080, People's Republic of China

- *PASCAL International Bibliography T205: Sciences de l' information Documentation,* INIST/CNRS-Service Gestion des Documents Primaires, 2, allee du Parc de Brabois, F-54514 Vandoeuvre-les-Nancy, Cedex, France

- *Periodica Islamica,* Berita Publishing, 22 Jalan Liku, 59100 Kuala Lumpur, Malaysia

- *Referativnyi Zhurnal (Abstracts Journal of the Institute of Scientific Information of the Republic of Russia),* The Institute of Scientific Information, Baltijskaja ul., 14, Moscow A-219, Republic of Russia

- *Social Science Citation Index* . . . . see: *Institute for Scientific Information*

- *Sociological Abstracts (SA),* Sociological Abstracts, Inc., P.O. Box 22206, San Diego, CA 92192-0206

(continued)

SPECIAL BIBLIOGRAPHIC NOTES

related to special journal issues (separates)
and indexing/abstracting

❑ indexing/abstracting services in this list will also cover material in any "separate" that is co-published simultaneously with Haworth's special thematic journal issue or DocuSerial. Indexing/abstracting usually covers material at the article/chapter level.

❑ monographic co-editions are intended for either non-subscribers or libraries which intend to purchase a second copy for their circulating collections.

❑ monographic co-editions are reported to all jobbers/wholesalers/approval plans. The source journal is listed as the "series" to assist the prevention of duplicate purchasing in the same manner utilized for books-in-series.

❑ to facilitate user/access services all indexing/abstracting services are encouraged to utilize the co-indexing entry note indicated at the bottom of the first page of each article/chapter/contribution.

❑ this is intended to assist a library user of any reference tool (whether print, electronic, online, or CD-ROM) to locate the monographic version if the library has purchased this version but not a subscription to the source journal.

❑ individual articles/chapters in any Haworth publication are also available through the Haworth Document Delivery Services (HDDS).

Serials Management in the Electronic Era: Papers in Honor of Peter Gellatly, Founding Editor of *The Serials Librarian*

CONTENTS

ALL HAWORTH BOOKS AND JOURNALS
ARE PRINTED ON CERTIFIED
ACID-FREE PAPER

ABOUT THE EDITORS

Jim Cole, MA, is Principal Serials Cataloger at Iowa State University in Ames. Among his research interests are European trends and practices in serials management. Mr. Cole is the author of a variety of scholarly articles, book reviews, and columns and is Co-editor of *Serials Cataloging: The State of the Art* (The Haworth Press, Inc., 1987) and *Serials Cataloging: Modern Perspectives and International Developments* (The Haworth Press, Inc., 1992). Editor of *The Serials Librarian,* he has served on several committees of the American Library Association and is a corresponding member of the Verein Deutscher Bibliothekare, the Association of German Librarians.

James W. Williams, MLS, Editor, is Assistant Education and Social Science Librarian and Cataloging Coordinator for the Social Sciences Division Libraries at the University of Illinois at Urbana-Champaign. He is the author of numerous technical services related articles and is Co-editor of *Serials Cataloging: Modern Perspectives and International Developments* (The Haworth Press, Inc., 1992). A member of the American Library Association, he has performed extensive committee service for the Association for Library Collections and Technical Services and the Association of College and Research Libraries.

Introduction

It is a truism that the advent of the computer and the proliferation of computing technology have altered many aspects of our lives and our work. Serials management, the business that we are about, has been transformed in the last several decades, changing in ways that all but the most farsighted could not have predicted. The papers contained herein are concerned with serials management as it has evolved–and continues to evolve–in the electronic era. The authors and editors of this collection dedicate it to Peter Gellatly with gratitude for his efforts on behalf of all those interested in the betterment of serials management today and in the future.

Following Ruth Carter's tribute to Peter, the collection opens with Stewart Shelline's discussion of the World Wide Web edition of the *Deseret News,* a Salt Lake City newspaper. This in turn is followed by "Network Accessed Scholarly Serials," in which Les Hawkins focuses on some of the collaborative efforts to publish serials and articles in the sciences and other disciplines in the network environment. Next is "Electronic Murmurs from the Desk of an Ink-Stained Wretch," by Joe Morehead, *The Serials Librarian*'s Government Serials Editor.

While electronic publications are transforming the library scene today, the use of computers in libraries in general is impacting how we work and what we accomplish, both in libraries and library schools. The next several articles concern themselves with various ways in which this is true. First, Libby Cooley and Edward Goedeken assert that libraries have an obligation to select, acquire, orga-

[Haworth co-indexing entry note]: "Introduction." Cole, Jim, and James W. Williams. Co-published simultaneously in *The Serials Librarian* (The Haworth Press, Inc.) Vol. 29, No. 3/4, 1996, pp. 1-3; and: *Serials Management in the Electronic Era: Papers in Honor of Peter Gellatly, Founding Editor of* The Serials Librarian (ed: Jim Cole, and James W. Williams) The Haworth Press, Inc., 1996, pp. 1-3. Single or multiple copies of this article are available for a fee from The Haworth Document Delivery Service [1-800-342-9678, 9:00 a.m. - 5:00 p.m. (EST). E-mail address: getinfo@haworth.com].

nize, and make information available in whatever format is appropriate for their users. F. Dixon Brooke, Jr. then examines the role of subscription or information agencies in the electronic era, and Suzanne Fedunok discusses progress regarding the implementation of proposals for interinstitutional serials cooperation at the SUNY Centers. Next William Loughner demonstrates how the CD-ROM version of the *Science Citation Index* can be used in conjunction with a personal computer to generate local citation analysis reports utilizing a much larger base of citations than was previously possible. Following this, Esther Bierbaum discusses instruction regarding electronic serials in the library and information science curriculum, and Martha Hruska presents a member's perspective of the CONSER Program. Mary Schlembach and William Mischo then describe a networked serials control system encompassing serials processing, public service, and end-user functions that has been developed at the Grainger Engineering Library Information Center at the University of Illinois at Urbana-Champaign.

Communication among library school students and serialists, like everything else, is changing. Several articles document some of the developments that are taking place. In the first of these articles, Kathryn Luther Henderson tells how practicing technical services librarians have successfully served as e-mail mentors in the Technical Services Functions course at the Graduate School of Library and Information Science at the University of Illinois at Urbana-Champaign. Next Joanne Gold, Information Officer with the BUBL Information Service, discusses this premier resource for both librarians and scholars. Jeanne Boydston then describes serials-related information on the World Wide Web, and Nancy De Sa gives advice on how to go about starting a WWW journal.

The collection concludes with two articles. In the first of these, Nancy Eaton offers insight into new challenges for technical services in the coming century. The final article, by Robert Cameron, describes a directory of computing science journals that he has developed which revolutionizes the concept of, and sets new standards for, serials directories.

As with any collection of papers, this has been a joint effort between the editors and the individual authors. The editors wish to thank all the authors for their participation in the development of *Serials Management in the Electronic Era*.

Jim Cole
James W. Williams
May 1996

Peter Gellatly–
Editor with a Deft Touch

Ruth C. Carter

One of life's pleasures is an opportunity to work with editor *par excellence,* Peter Gellatly. Soft spoken and master of the gentle nudge, he personifies the seven P's of a good editor's traits: persistence, persuasion, promptness, perception (the ability to identify good topics and talented individuals), patience, praise, and personal interest in his colleagues. Of course, one can toss in some other necessary traits like flexibility, generosity, a sense of humor, and the ability to take disappointments with grace. The latter is important, for example, when all those manuscripts you had expected fail to materialize, or publications are delayed, or another journal scoops your planned topics.

Peter's career as an editor is by no means his first. In fact it is not even second. Born in Scotland, Peter saw active duty in World War II in an aircrew position in the Royal Canadian Air Force. Following the war he served in a confidential governmental capacity in Ottawa before moving to the West Coast and the University of British Columbia. There he received his BA in 1950 with a major in languages. Turning toward professional pursuits, Peter earned his Master's degree in Library Science at the University of

Ruth C. Carter is Editor of *Cataloging & Classification Quarterly.* She is currently Curator, Darlington Library, University of Pittsburgh, Pittsburgh, PA 15260. E-mail: rcc13@vms.cis.pitt.edu.

[Haworth co-indexing entry note]: "Peter Gellatly–Editor with a Deft Touch." Carter, Ruth C. Co-published simultaneously in *The Serials Librarian* (The Haworth Press, Inc.) Vol. 29, No. 3/4, 1996, pp. 5-8; and: *Serials Management in the Electronic Era: Papers in Honor of Peter Gellatly, Founding Editor of* The Serials Librarian (ed: Jim Cole, and James W. Williams) The Haworth Press, Inc., 1996, pp. 5-8. Single or multiple copies of this article are available for a fee from The Haworth Document Delivery Service [1-800-342-9678, 9:00 a.m. - 5:00 p.m. (EST). E-mail address: getinfo@haworth.com].

Washington in 1954. His library degree and facility with languages got him into acquisitions and collection development at the University of Washington where he had a distinguished twenty-three years, first as Head Bibliographer and later as Head of the Serials Division. During those years Peter participated actively in the Pacific Northwest Library Association and the American Library Association. He served on numerous committees and frequently made presentations. While at Washington he served as a consultant to two large American subscription agencies and was articles editor of the now defunct *Cigar Magazine.* Peter also became involved with publishing as co-author of the *Guide to Serial Subscription Agencies* and as the author of many articles. He also briefly returned to Ottawa on two breaks from Washington. On one occasion he served as a cataloger at the Library of Parliament; during the other he had a stint as a reference librarian at Algonquin College.

Peter left the University of Washington permanently when only fifty-five to devote himself to editing. He became the first editor of *The Serials Librarian* for The Haworth Press, Inc., and found his niche. The rest as they say "is history." His accomplishments as a journal editor are public record: twenty-six volumes of *The Serials Librarian,* three volumes of *Technical Services Quarterly,* at least sixteen of *Collection Management,* plus five or more volumes of both *Library and Archival Security* and *Behavioral and Social Sciences Librarianship* not to mention eight monographic volumes. But Peter's responsibilities do not end with serving as Editor of specific journals. His talents have earned him the position of Editor-in-Chief for all the Haworth Press library science journals. In that capacity he keeps tabs on all the Haworth library science publishing and gets actively involved in identifying new editors as necessary or potential new initiatives. His responsibilities also include editing Haworth's Series on Library and Information Science.

My own experience with Peter began when I submitted a series of articles on the development of the Pennsylvania Union List of Serials (PaULS) to *The Serials Librarian* over the course of several years in the early 1980s. You can imagine how stunned I was when Peter called one day in 1984 and asked me if I would be willing to edit *Cataloging & Classification Quarterly*. This was certainly something I had never thought about, yet Peter had the perception to figure out that I would like it. Since that time, more than a decade ago, I have had the opportunity to benefit from Peter's guidance and insights in any number of ways. Let me share a few with you.

Many new editors have a hard time getting a flow of manuscripts established. Here Peter helped by directing a couple of manuscripts to me at an early date. At the same time he wrote (1985) that he had not yet hooked up his Apple computer, but expected to do so soon. Meanwhile, he kept in close touch with my progress on my first couple of issues. Peter provided both the gentle encouragement and helpful clarifications in procedures that were needed to get past the critical initial stages. But, above all, Peter supplied necessary support and his quiet vote of confidence.

Many of Peter's letters comment on the weather which in Seattle was often rain. Or he talks about his cats, the crocuses blooming in his yard, weeding petunias, health and family, or travel or plans for moving. *The Serials Librarian* and Peter's other fine journals have been put together alternately in Seattle and in various Canadian locations. Whatever hardships moving has brought Peter, they were transparent, or very nearly so, to his authors and readers.

Peter once described his editing as being carried out "in solitary splendor"–or perhaps "grumpy solitude." Like other editors, however, Peter is not alone. No one knows better than he that producing a journal or monograph is teamwork between the authors, editor, publisher, editorial board members, column editors, and production staff. One never knows exactly what the next mail, telephone call, fax, or e-mail will bring. All involved expect prompt attention and deserve prompt attention. Peter has unfailingly provided it along with many times the communications that deepen into personal as well as professional interests. And, the resulting publications touch many readers now and into the future. Peter's accomplishments are most impressive for this his third and probably best "career."

That Peter has done so well and touched so many people, is amply demonstrated by his recognition as the recipient of the 1995 Bowker/Ulrich's Serials Librarianship Award and now by the many willing contributors to this Festschrift. In recent years, with a decade of editing behind me, I can often answer my own questions and, therefore, haven't turned to Peter as often as in the past. Yet Peter always will be an inspiration for me and for the many others he has helped and encouraged in writing or editing. Peter Gellatly is a consummate editor, a valued colleague, and trusted mentor. Peter, all the best!

The *Deseret News* Web Edition

Stewart E. Shelline

SUMMARY. The *Deseret News*, a daily newspaper in Salt Lake City, Utah, with a circulation of 66,000, confronted a variety of challenges before launching a digital edition on the World Wide Web in September 1995.

This article is a description of the thinking that went into the decision to go online as well as the consequences of that decision. It also describes the process the *Deseret News* uses to move articles and photos from its publishing systems onto the Web, and issues regarding the archiving of digital information. *[Article copies available for a fee from The Haworth Document Delivery Service: 1-800-342-9678. E-mail address: getinfo@haworth.com]*

Three years after Brigham Young led Mormon pioneers to the Salt Lake Valley in 1847, the first issue of the Deseret News *was pulled off a small hand-cranked press. This eight-page newspaper was the first published in what was then called the territory of Deseret. Although the state of Utah has long-since replaced the old territory, the* Deseret News *retains its original name and is published daily as Utah's oldest newspaper.*

–From the *Deseret News* Web Edition

Stewart E. Shelline is Director of Online Services for Deseret News Publishing Co., 135 Regent Street, Salt Lake City, UT 84110. E-mail: stewart@desnews.com.

[Haworth co-indexing entry note]: "The *Deseret News* Web Edition." Shelline, Stewart E. Co-published simultaneously in *The Serials Librarian* (The Haworth Press, Inc.) Vol. 29, No. 3/4, 1996, pp. 9-18; and: *Serials Management in the Electronic Era: Papers in Honor of Peter Gellatly, Founding Editor of The Serials Librarian* (ed: Jim Cole, and James W. Williams) The Haworth Press, Inc., 1996, pp. 9-18. Single or multiple copies of this article are available for a fee from The Haworth Document Delivery Service [1-800-342-9678, 9:00 a.m. - 5:00 p.m. (EST). E-mail address: getinfo@haworth.com].

When the Mormon pioneers entered the Salt Lake Valley 149 years ago, they found themselves in the heart of a wild, untracked frontier. Today, the newspaper they started is on the edge of a new and entirely different frontier: the World Wide Web. It is a frontier not of mountains and rivers and trees, but of bits and browsers and hypertext.

In the process of producing a digital edition, the *Deseret News* has confronted myriad challenges common to a medium attempting to move from the tangible world of ink and paper to the transitory world of bits, the DNA of digital communications.

The story of our digital dabbling really began in late 1993, when we began developing our own dial-up online service. We had looked at the various BBS programs, such as PCBoard, Galacticomm, Wildcat, etc., and found them all lacking in ease of use and overall presentation. America Online had raised the bar dramatically by emphasizing the ease of its interface and raising the level of design found in online services (the World Wide Web was still an obscure phenomenon). We also knew that AOL, Compuserve, and Prodigy were not looking for partnerships with newspapers of our size. But we didn't want to sacrifice presentation by going with a text-based system or the crude graphics of RIP-based BBS software. After much discussion, we decided the best course would be to develop our own software.

In late 1993, after our management had agreed to spend money to research our proposal for an online service, we prepared a demo version of our software. After focus groups in Utah and Southern California (where there is a large LDS population) confirmed our decision, the *Deseret News* created the position of Director of Online Services and allocated funds for the purchase of the necessary server, PCs, and modems. In May 1994, programming began in earnest. Nine months later, in February 1995, we released the first version of the software.

Our research indicated that we could expect one to two percent of our subscriber base would pay a monthly fee to receive the *Deseret News* online. For us, this meant around 900 subscribers by the end of the first year. All of our development was done with this in mind, but at the last minute management decided to offer the service for free, as a value-added feature of the newspaper itself, rather than charge a subscription fee. As a result, we found ourselves swamped in the first few weeks. I was working late on the day we announced Crossroads in the paper. At about 5 p.m., when the paper is delivered, our phone began to ring. And ring. By the time the calls slowed down, a week or so later, nearly 4,000 people had requested the free software.

Of course, we weren't prepared for this onslaught. But it confirmed our belief that subscribers were willing to try new technology and owned the computers and modems to do so. Most important of all, it put in place a structure that allowed us to get on the Web in a surprisingly easy and low-cost way a few months later.

The core of this structure is a collection of programs we call the Gateway. Its job is to take the various articles from the newspaper and strip out the pieces needed for digital publication, such as the headline, byline, text, photo credits, etc., and store them in a relational database. Once in this database, articles can easily and rapidly be reassembled for different online products—our own online service, the Web, CD-ROM, etc. But this process is anything but simple.

Over the years, the *Deseret News* has created a rich set of formatting commands—some 500 at last count—to allow editors and designers to produce the precise look desired for a given article. This offers tremendous flexibility when the final result is a printed document, but it becomes a burden when attempting to re-purpose the document for online publication or archiving. Thus, much of the effort we have put into the Gateway has been in undoing what the editors and designers have done. This process is also highly prone to error—multiple commands exist to accomplish essentially the same effect; commands can easily be misspelled or may lack required terminating characters, making it difficult to accurately extract certain pieces.

From the beginning, it was clear the Online Services department would not be able to produce its electronic products using a large staff. We would have to automate as much of the process as possible. As a result, several concepts guided our development of the Gateway:

1. Wherever possible, we would maintain a single copy of any document during production (any information needed to publish the document online would have to be included in the document itself).
2. Any information we added to the document could not affect the regular print production process.
3. Publication online would be defined as occurring at the point an article is released by the copy desk. This was the only event reliable enough to ensure that everything moved to the online edition. It also gave us the advantage of moving copy throughout a 5-6 hour period, rather than in a single batch after the paper itself was finished. This was important because we are an evening paper–publishing earlier allowed us to compete with the morning paper.
4. The process couldn't cost much in terms of equipment, software, or labor.

The first step was to develop a system of classification. Because grouping was no longer constrained by space, we could organize our online edition any way we felt was most appropriate to the medium. The printed *Deseret News* is generally produced in four sections: World and national news, local news, sports, and features. Business news is included in the sports section and the editorial/oped pages in the world/nation section. We spent weeks trying to decide if maintaining this organization made sense in an online edition, or if we should take a knife to this organization and carve out entirely new sections. Ultimately, however, we decided to take advantage of a structure familiar to our readers and kept the same basic organization as the paper.

We then assigned each of these sections a keyword (WIR for world/nation, CIT for local, SPT for sports, etc.) and asked each section editor to create keywords for the major categories their desk covered. For example, the sports desk came up with sub-classifications corresponding to the major professional sports (NBA, NFL, AL, NL, etc.). Once these were set, we asked the editors to begin including these keywords in the header of every article. This information is then passed on from the publishing system to the Gateway, which uses it to determine how to process each document and where to store it for Crossroads as well as the Web page.

Another significant problem that had to be solved was associating articles with photos. For the print edition, this association takes place when the pages are electronically composed and relies entirely on the skills of the composer (whom we call a paginator), since there is no hard link between the document and the photo. The paginator knows the name of the article and the name of the photo and knows where to put them, but there is no way for this connection to be made without human involvement. To solve this problem, we asked the paginators (who design the pages on paper and then later assemble all the pieces on page makeup stations) to begin embedding the information needed to associate documents and photos. The Gateway then uses this information to marry the various pieces and store them in the database.

About 90 to 95 percent of the documents that are published each day in the paper make it to the database without any human intervention. The remaining 5 to 10 percent don't arrive for various reasons: improper coding, missing photos, etc. Some articles, usually part of graphics-rich section covers, are produced on Macintosh computers and don't enter the publishing system until after the pagination stage. These articles are moved into the database separately as one of the responsibilities of our online editor and assistant.

Once the problems involved in tapping into the regular production stream were solved for Crossroads, re-purposing that content for the Web was an easy step. In fact, it took us little more than an afternoon to develop the site itself, although we had done a significant amount of work designing the look and feel of the pages beforehand. We wrote a small program to take the documents as they arrived at the database and, using the design we had created, wrote them out to our Web server in HTML.

The *Deseret News* Web Edition (http://www.desnews.com) began in September 1995. We use Netscape Commerce Server running on a Sun Sparc/20 with 4GB of storage and 64MB RAM. Static documents and CGI scripts are cached on the Sparc, while articles and photos are retrieved through a read-only connection to a Novell network. We are linked to the Internet via a T1 connection through Electric Lightwave Inc. Our archives exist in a Vu/Text SAVE database maintained on an IBM RS6000 running AIX and linked to our Web site's search page via in-house software.

We publish the entire *Deseret News* print edition, including photos, on Crossroads and in the Web Edition. Stories are published online beginning at 7 a.m. each day and continuing through 3 p.m., and again from around 6 p.m. to 10 p.m. We also publish an online edition of the *LDS Church News* (http://www.desnews.com/cn), a weekly newsmagazine for members of the LDS Church, each Saturday.

Why did we decide to produce an electronic edition of the *Deseret News*? While it is tempting to answer "Because we could," there were more substantive reasons for our decision. First among these is to remain competitive in our market. The *Deseret News* is the evening paper in Salt Lake City and competes not only with the morning paper, but now with all other media outlets as well. In that environment, our goal is not just to maintain our position as a producer of textual and graphical material, but to expand into areas not traditionally part of print media, such as real-time information and audio and video. While the nature of our competition has changed as a result of the Web, our commitment to be the dominant news and information provider in our market has not.

Unfortunately, because the *Deseret News* is part of a Joint Operating Agreement with the morning paper, we are unable to deliver display and classified advertising electronically to our subscribers. The Newspaper Agency Corp., which handles these functions for both newspapers under the JOA, is struggling to deliver solutions but has so far been unable to do so.

Another key reason we are on the Web is to conduct the research and development needed to familiarize ourselves with this technology and be able to take advantage of it. Until recently, newspapers were in the business of putting ink on paper. Once that was accomplished, we threw away everything we'd done and started over. Then, in the early 1980s, many newspapers began archiving at least the text of each issue. Some even archive the photos and graphics as well. At the *Deseret News*, we have maintained an electronic archive since April 1988, but we do not keep an integrated archive of text and photos. Additionally, our production equipment, such as the Atex terminals, the III pagination system, etc., are from an era in which "re-purposing" did not exist. As such, they present serious roadblocks to the kind of integrated newsroom I see as essential to the success of online publications. Our production process relies almost entirely on the skills of paginators to ensure that all the pieces on a page are assembled in the right way at the right time. Very little computer power is spent on ensuring data integrity, on structuring data in such a way that can easily be reused online. Part of our venture into online services is to confront the weaknesses of our current production process and find solutions.

We also can expand coverage and meet the needs of specific subscribers. Because an electronic newspaper is not constrained by space–the usual factor defining the amount of news in a given edition–we are able to "flesh out" a given story with background information and graphics and links to other sites for even more information. We can create highly focused editions, or pages, on topics of interest to our readers.

Perhaps the biggest advantage the Web Edition has over its paper counterpart is its sense of immediacy. Unlike many electronic newspapers, which update their pages once a day, the *Deseret News* Web Edition updates throughout the production cycle. In most cases, online readers see the news before it makes it to the press, which, in our market, means an 8-10 hour advantage. In addition, our online editors refresh the news once in the evening. In the past, when the Utah Jazz played a night game, *Deseret News* readers wouldn't be able to read about it until the following evening. Now, by reading the Web Edition, they can have game summaries and full stories within minutes of the game's end.

The Web Edition can also offer greater depth and breadth to a particular story. Background material that rarely makes it into the paper, such as the full text of a speech or press release, can be put on the Web Edition without regard to space limitations.

We also hoped to attract a younger audience, one that was used to retrieving news and information online. Interestingly, however, we are finding that many of our online readers are also in the "older" age group–a fast-growing (and unexpected) group of computer users.

An intriguing aspect of our experience has been the popularity of our archives. Second only to the *Deseret News* home page itself, articles retrieved from our archives are the most frequently requested item. On a typical day, for example, more than 900 documents are retrieved from our archives. One reason for this popularity may be that the *Deseret News* has a long-standing arrangement with the State of Utah to offer this archive to all public schools and government agencies in the state. In return, the state pays for some of the infrastructure costs for this access, which we also deliver via Telnet and dial-up BBS. Through this arrangement, libraries and other agencies are freed from the need to archive our newspaper themselves, lowering their costs and ensuring that those who lack the equipment to connect to the Web themselves can still do so through public institutions.

Although our archives have proven popular, they have also exposed serious weaknesses and forced us to think about how we manage our information. In the past, the *Deseret News* has maintained separate text and photo archives, with no connection between them. The text archive uses a very powerful search engine but is weakened by a lack of consistent classification and quirky storage decisions–all headlines are in upper case, for example, making it impossible to convert them back to the newspaper's downstyle. The photo archive is not comprehensive and suffers from a weak search engine and unstructured classification. Something as simple as including the caption with a photo is difficult because the caption must be typed in, since there is no link to the text archive (which does contain the caption but no reference to the photograph!).

Equally important is the relative lack of accessibility to these archives from the newsroom. We use some two dozen different hardware and software platforms to produce the *Deseret News*– most of which don't talk to each other or do so only in very primitive ways. When our online editor decides to produce a new product, he may spend the lion's share of his time just moving from terminal to terminal to get the documents and images he needs.

In response to this miasma, we are creating an "integrated archive" within the Online Services Department that will offer "one-seat" access to all of the *Deseret News* archives. Within this system, all of the items used to create an article–text, photos, hypertext links, etc.–will be treated as objects, to borrow a concept from computer programming. As an object, an article, for example, will have various attributes, such as a headline, byline, and text. More complex classes of documents can be created from this base class.

For example, a subclass of the base class may contain attributes for a photo reference and caption or hypertext link. Attributes for font, font size, font style, justification, columns, etc., will also be included.

In addition to attributes, an object will also have an associated set of events that trigger specific actions when they occur. For example, an event that modifies the document's text property might also cause a backup copy of the object to be created. Everything that affects a given object is contained within the object itself, dramatically reducing the overall complexity of the archival process and allowing editors to make changes without needing to know everything about the entire production process. Also, changes to a parent class are replicated through all subclasses, making object maintenance much more simple.

Our hope is that by creating this integrated archive we will be able to take advantage of the information we already have and be well-positioned for new opportunities.

In the ferocious pace of the information technology revolution, the *Deseret News'* brief participation still spans most of that revolution's history. We have accomplished most of the goals we set for ourselves: to remain competitive in our market; to understand the hurdles of digital publication; to expand our coverage of the news. But really, we're at the very beginning. Most of the exploration is still ahead. No one really knows to what extent consumers will be willing to pay for the services that will be offered on the Web. Many predict that the Web will not reach the general consumer market for years, if ever. But our goal is not to subject our fate to any particular medium, but to be ready to take advantage of whatever technology brings.

We don't believe online editions will replace print editions in the near future, though we believe the potential is there. For the time being, the two types of editions are complementary: After a hard day's work, the print edition is nice to curl up to. It is passive, compact, multiuser, and user-friendly. On the other hand, it doesn't archive well, gets ink on your hands, destroys trees, and comes only once a day. The online edition is ready when you are, contains more news than your paper, and lets you find articles from years ago. It is pro-active, customizable, easily shared, and organic. It also requires an expensive computer, patience with software and modems, and a chair.

Printed newspapers have significant long-term challenges: They are produced from a limited resource (trees), require expensive machinery and infrastructure to produce, and increasingly are perceived as irrelevant by young readers. However, it will take many years and many billions of dollars to develop the network and technology to deliver low-cost, interactive, high-speed digital newspapers to inexpensive devices. Until then, printed newspapers have an important—indeed, a dominant—role in the delivery of low-cost, broad news and information.

Network Accessed Scholarly Serials

Les Hawkins

SUMMARY. Commercial publishers, scholarly societies, platform providers, and libraries are collaborating on experiments to provide scholarly serials and articles on the Internet and other networks. Some of the models for collaboration include the preprint database and the digital library. Other commercial publishers of scholarly serials are quickly moving to provide electronic versions of material previously only issued in print and to develop new products entirely in electronic form. *[Article copies available for a fee from The Haworth Document Delivery Service: 1-800-342-9678. E-mail address: getinfo@haworth.com]*

A number of people and organizations are attempting to solve the problems of delivering scholarly information on the Internet and other networks. These include individual scholars, commercial publishers, university presses, volunteer academic-based serial publishers, and libraries. Increasingly these actors are collaborating in various combinations to experiment with user interfaces, file processing, and archiving scholarly material. While there are a number of popular commercial network based serials publishing efforts,[1] this article will focus on some of the collaborative efforts to publish serials and articles in the sciences and other disciplines in a network environment.

Les Hawkins is a cataloger at the U.S. ISSN Center, National Serials Data Program, Library of Congress, Washington, DC 20540-4160.

The views expressed in this paper do not necessarily reflect those of the Library of Congress.

[Haworth co-indexing entry note]: "Network Accessed Scholarly Serials." Hawkins, Les. Co-published simultaneously in *The Serials Librarian* (The Haworth Press, Inc.) Vol. 29, No. 3/4, 1996, pp. 19-31; and: *Serials Management in the Electronic Era: Papers in Honor of Peter Gellatly, Founding Editor of* The Serials Librarian (ed: Jim Cole, and James W. Williams) The Haworth Press, Inc., 1996, pp. 19-31. Single or multiple copies of this article are available for a fee from The Haworth Document Delivery Service [1-800-342-9678, 9:00 a.m. - 5:00 p.m. (EST). E-mail address: getinfo@haworth.com].

EARLY DEVELOPMENTS

Lancaster and others have outlined the history of computer processing in serials publishing.[2] This history goes back some thirty years and includes, at the beginning, steps to process information in the production of print journals, indexing tools, and online databases such as Medline. During the late 1970s several experimental projects were focused on providing researchers in closed electronic networks with journal articles and other online communication. The Electronic Information Exchange System (EIES) and the Birmingham and Loughborough Electronic Network Development (BLEND) both produced networked electronic journals. These experiments together demonstrated features such as peer review, article archiving, and reader feedback mechanisms. These experiments were of short duration, and users experienced difficulty viewing articles with the computer and telecommunication equipment of the late 1970s and early 1980s. Text was limited to ASCII characters and readers often preferred printing out material for reading rather than viewing on the screen. Another difficulty was attracting writers willing to publish in a medium not entirely sanctioned by academic tenure review standards.

An early hypertext journal, *HyperBIT,* was produced in 1990 as part of Project QUARTET which provided users with hypertext links between related articles, pop-up windows with bibliographic information about references, and the ability to display graphics, sound, and animation.[3] A problem encountered by users of *HyperBIT* was low screen resolution. Graphics were not rendered well on-screen; the print version of this publication was a much better format for presenting graphic information.

The designers of these projects had in mind some features of electronic scholarly publishing which are beginning to be realized by publishers of networked serials today. Some of these include:

1. Immediacy of article delivery, with the option of delivering single articles without waiting to compile several into an issue.
2. Peer reviewed forums where scholars can depend on the integrity of research and the database of articles archived.

3. Reader feedback mechanisms which provide a collaborative atmosphere for the development of final published products and the ability to distinguish finished works from preprint material.
4. Hypertext links to related articles in a database and to references.
5. The ability to display graphics which include complex figures and the ability to present multimedia files.
6. The ability to search text with controlled or full text capability.

Some of the problems faced in these early experiments also have plagued the development of fully networked electronic journals. These include:

1. Technological or software roadblocks which make viewing text or graphics on screen difficult for the end user. The display of complex graphics and multimedia material often requires the end user to have the right equipment and software. Additionally, multimedia material requires a larger network bandwidth before it can be easily handled online.
2. Difficulty attracting writers willing to publish in a new medium lacking the proven ability to maintain the high standards of editorial quality, peer review, copy editing, and intellectual integrity accorded the products of commercial print publishers by academic employers.
3. Long term funding commitments for high quality editorial functions, some of which include coordinating peer review, copyediting, and guaranteeing the archival record.

Typically early online serials of the late 1980s and early 1990s were published by volunteer academic publishers rather than commercial publishers and ranged from peer reviewed scholarly journals like the *Public-Access Computer Systems Review, Psycoloquy, Ejournal,* and *Postmodern Culture* to newsletter type publications. Until recently, the large majority of these networked serials were distributed primarily by e-mail or retrievable by ftp and later gopher. In the early 1990s several scientific societies and commercial publishers began to make plans for experimenting with electronic serials using these delivery and access methods.[4] Often these plans included parallel publishing with existing print titles, as a way of easing into full production of electronic products. Commercial publishers began to experiment with scanning print titles for delivery on CD-ROM, which was the most powerful delivery mechanism for scanned images at the time (and today for multimedia files). Some publishers made ASCII versions of their titles, generally partial contents of the print versions, available on commercial databases like Dialogue.

CLIENT SERVER MODEL

Publishers of Internet distributed serials began to provide a variety of file formats for entire articles or parts of articles (those providing graphic information) for downloading or printing. Adobe's portable document format (pdf), TeX for handling of complex mathematical figures, and PostScript offered users of serials a variety of viewing and printing options. Single articles published as an entire issue speeded access to completely reviewed and copy-edited work (a tradition begun in print publishing) became more common, though issue designation and page or paragraph numbering for citation purposes was not abandoned. Articles were compiled into searchable databases of completed articles making use of listserv software and client server protocols (ftp and gopher) to allow their search and retrieval. The listserv model of distribution sometimes provided subscribers with a contents notification of current issues, with abstracts. Readers were then able to decide which article to retrieve and what format or delivery method was appropriate. Many of these features of earlier networked serials have been carried on and embellished in the current World Wide Web environment.

For example, the electronic version of *Astrophysical Journal Letters* section (*ApJL*)[5] published by the University of Chicago Press for the American Astrophysical Society can be accessed by the World Wide Web and read online in the Hypertext Markup Language (HTML) version. However, since HTML does not render complex figures or mathematical notation well (they are provided in linked image files in the HTML version), readers are encouraged to download the pdf article files for viewing or printing, because they provide the best resolution and are the exact files used to produce the print version. Articles are compiled into a searchable database with a Web-based client interface.

HYPERTEXT AND DATABASES

HTML is a mixture of structural markup and display specification and is therefore limited in its ability to provide complete logical markup of documents. It does, however, make possible a uniform, network-wide platform for authoring and publishing on the World Wide Web. Hypertext Transport Protocol (HTTP) allows the type of hypertext linking examined in the HyperBIT experiment. Hypertext linking on the World Wide Web permits creators of online serials to link to other parts of a document, bibliographic citations and other networked documents. Associated databases of articles can ensure availability and authenticity of peer reviewed material if there is a commitment to archival maintenance. Article databases can also be structured to store feedback from reader comments and make them available for consideration alongside a preprint or final version. The blending of hypertext linking and databases of related articles and documents allows citation tracing in both a forward and backward direction, providing the reader with a document's bibliographic context in the desktop environment. In databases that provide articles in text searchable formats, search engines present a variety of text and controlled search options of document portions (e.g., abstract, table of contents), other documents or databases.

Preprint Database Models

The rise in serial acquisition costs has for a long time fueled an interest among academic institutions in taking advantage of network-based publishing initiatives. There has been hope that electronic serials and other resources would be less costly than print materials. The success and proliferation of preprint databases in the fields of physics and mathematics have provided incentive to others interested in establishing low cost, high transaction preprint databases in other fields. In some ways these efforts demonstrate a way to circumvent the traditional commercial route of scholarly publishing while providing access to current research, though in a sometimes unrefereed environment. It has been pointed out that building in a feedback mechanism for commentary from reputable practitioners and making clear distinctions between preprint and final product can help maintain the reliability and scholarly integrity of material stored in preprint databases.[6]

The Los Alamos e-print archives, covering several physics disciplines, represents a model of electronic publishing that bypasses the costs of typesetting, marketing, and editorial coordination traditionally performed by commercial science publishers. It typifies preprint databases in that it accepts voluntarily contributed articles which are added to the archive database in a prescribed format such as TeX. E-mail notifications of new articles and abstracts are sent to subscribers, or users can search the database through gopher or World Wide Web interfaces. Users then download desired articles. Since its beginning in 1991, the Los Alamos archive has become an important research tool in physics and handles over 50,000 transactions daily.

Michael Harnard, publisher of the electronic journal *Psycoloquy* has recently obtained a grant to establish the Cognitive Sciences Eprint Archive at the University of Southhampton in England. It will follow the Los Alamos model but will focus on the behavioral and cognitive sciences. Harnard has mentioned that authors in these fields will need encouragement to deposit material, so that a useful mass of articles can be developed in the database.[7]

InterJournal was developed as part of the New England Complex Systems Institute. It is a preprint database for articles in three specialized science and engineering fields.[8] It includes an "open refereeing" feature in which referees register and choose which articles to review. This is intended to provide diversity in the review and feedback authors receive. Public comments are also solicited and made available, as are the reports of referees. *InterJournal* makes clear distinctions between preprint and fully refereed articles and even provides links to abstracts of rejected items.

PRINT SERIALS ONLINE

The graphical user interface of Web browsers provides the ability to display files in graphic formats, a bit-mapped image of an entire scanned print serial, for example, or a link to a graphic file which contains a figure referred to in a text. Publishers of existing print serials are experimenting with providing readers with the scanned images of print serials to enhance on-screen viewing or printing. In some cases they are also simultaneously indexing the serial in parallel text files, increasingly marked up in Standard Generalized Markup Language (SGML) to provide search capabilities and a logical document structure. Similarly, multi-media files are available via graphical Web browsers, though currently widespread use of multimedia files on the Internet is hampered by low network band-width and the need for users to mount and maintain additional software necessary to view graphic files or hear audio files.

THE DIGITAL LIBRARY MODEL

The digital library is a model for several projects delivering scholarly articles in specialized subject fields. It frequently involves digitizing print material, but includes documents originally in digitized form. The efforts described below involve collaboration between one or more organizations. These can include commercial publishers or scholarly societies (frequently with a primarily print catalog), technical/platform providers (providing software, delivery platforms and technical publishing assistance), academic departments or government agencies with a specialized subject focus, and libraries. The digital library model is aimed at delivering a rich database of resources, discovery capabilities, and document delivery to users in an institutional or campus environment.

Project Muse

Project Muse is a collaboration between Johns Hopkins University Press, Homewood Academic Computing, and the Milton S. Eisenhower Library. Plans include providing online access to more than 40 journals from the Hopkins catalog in the humanities and social sciences over a three year period which began in 1995. A permanent archive of the online issues will be maintained with the possibility of adding back issues sometime later. New issues for the online journals will be made available approximately four weeks in advance of the print version. The on-screen viewing platform based on HTML allows access to some image files of graphic material appearing in the print versions. Access to these files depends on the Project obtaining appropriate permissions from the copyright owners of images for online display. The HTML platform also enables registered users to easily printout material which is liberally supported by the Muse licensing agreement. Audio and video file access is also a possibility, though so far none of the journals published contains such material. Table of contents, abstracts, full text and cross journal searching are supported. Controlled indexing via Library of Congress Subject Headings is provided by catalogers at the Eisenhower Library and the electronic journals have been assigned unique ISSN.

Licensing is geared toward consortia of libraries or entire campuses and institutions. Subscribing organizations are provided access to the MUSE file server by the Internet domain name so that all users at a site are provided access to the journals subscribed to. Libraries are encouraged to add "hot links" via Uniform Resource Locators (URLs) in local catalogs if they are able to block access from outside users. For "partner" libraries subscribing to all journals added to the database in 1996, the project will provide journal use statistics for the library's subdomains. This could provide a library useful information in deciding which MUSE journals to subscribe to in the future. Members of the "subscriber community" are permitted to download, print, make unlimited copies for personal or classroom use, and archive, including conversion to another medium.[9]

Red Sage

Red Sage Digital Library Project is a collaboration between Springer-Verlag, University of California, San Francisco (UCSF) Library Center for Knowledge Management, and AT&T Bell Laboratories. The project is delivering 70 Springer-Verlag journals online to the UCSF medical school campus using AT&T Bell Laboratories' RightPages image-based viewing software. RightPages is designed to provide a pleasing user display on-screen with a print-like interface for text, figures and other graphics. The interface allows for browsing of journal titles as if they were arranged on a library shelf. Full text searching in underlying text files is also available. An interesting feature of the software is the user profiling and notification which alerts the user to new articles matching a preselected interest profile.

As of fall of 1995, plans for Red Sage included accepting journal titles coded in SGML from several other commercial and society publishers and a World Wide Web version.[10]

OCLC Electronic Journals Online

The OCLC Electronic Journals Online (EJO) service takes advantage of development efforts by OCLC in the past several years in delivering the specialized science journal *Online Journal of Current Clinical Trials*. This journal began as a joint effort of OCLC and the American Association for the Advancement of Science in 1992. It is now owned by Chapman Hall and still available as part of the EJO service. It features advanced windowing facilities, permitting users to view related text without leaving the page. It also features hypertext linking to external databases such as Medline for display of abstracts of cited articles.[11] Early on, the journal suffered from problems encountered by other early electronic journals in attracting authors willing to publish in a non-print medium.[12] Recently, OCLC announced plans to provide access to 60 science journals from 11 different publishers.[13] OCLC thus provides a platform for publishers interested in experimenting with electronic formats in a uniform environment that speeds publication of material. It also allows interactivity (electronic letters to the editor, for example) and the mounting of supplemental data that usually would not be included in print format journals. Increasing the number of individual publishers, and journals, as well as links to external sources expands the database of articles to which users have access. It may also have a legitimizing effect, encouraging authors and the academic tenure system to have more confidence in the electronic medium, since many of the publishers involved have a solid reputation for scholarly publishing.

TORPEDO

The Optical Retrieval Project: Electronic Documents Online (TORPEDO) is a collaboration between the Ruth H. Hooker

Research Library of the Naval Research Laboratory (NRL) and the American Physical Society to deliver articles from *Physical Review Letters* and *Physical Review E* and a number of other documents to researchers at NRL.[14] Access is limited to NRL staff and contractors and permits online viewing and printing. Contents of the journals from January 1994 are being stored both as image and text files to facilitate online viewing and searching. The Library is experimenting with providing SGML versions and viewers capable of handling SGML. Another aspect of the project is to provide access to back issues of *Physical Review A, B, C,* and *D* on the Physical Review On-Line Archive (PROLA), in cooperation with the Los Alamos National Laboratory. Currently only ASCII format is available, though scanned images are expected to be part of the PROLA database.

COMMERCIAL PUBLISHING EFFORTS

The popularity of the World Wide Web as a commercial venue has coincided with falling library subscriptions to print serials and the visibility of some of the digital library projects mentioned above. This has provided a motivation for commercial publishers to experiment seriously with providing value-added features to electronic serials and to try unique subscription and licensing agreements. For commercial publishers of scholarly serials, this has also led to collaborations with a variety of other entities involved with publishing. Some are collaborating with platform providers such as OCLC, as noted above. Such collaborations have allowed publishers to evaluate user requirements for value-added features, demand for electronic products, pricing structure, production costs, security, and access issues. Often these publishers have begun their efforts with providing electronic versions from their print catalog and have moved to providing a limited number of purely electronic serials.

Elsevier is collaborating with several academic institutions to provide specialized subject area journals to test costing and delivery models in The University Licensing Program (TULIP).[15] Participating institutions receive the journal content from Elsevier and incorporate it into local delivery systems, which varies depending on how institutions implement access. Elsevier is also delivering two fully electronic journals, *Gene-COMBIS* and *New Astronomy*. *Gene-COMBIS* provides a unique feature that allows users to download programs and data accompanying articles and replicate the analyses outlined in the research.[16]

Academic Press has plans to offer 178 of its journals in 1996 via the World Wide Web with a program called International Digital Electronic Access Library (IDEAL).[17] It is aimed at library consortia or networks and will allow licensed users to view, print, and download articles in Adobe Acrobat format. The licensing agreement prohibits systematic or "massive" downloading of articles for database manipulation or archiving. Academic plans to allow unlicensed users to search the database of tables of contents and abstracts (IDEAL home page). The number of online journals that consortia members are allowed to access is based on the number of print subscriptions. This allows some consortia members with few Academic Press print subscriptions online access to a larger number of online journals.

John Wiley has been publishing the fully electronic *Journal of Image Guided Surgery* since the spring of 1995. This journal has featured video clips of surgical procedures. Another new electronic-only product from Wiley is the *Electronic Journal of Theoretical Chemistry (EJTC)*, a specialized peer-reviewed journal. Like many commercial publishers, Wiley provides limited access to non-subscribers for demonstration purposes.[18]

Beginning in 1996, Taylor & Francis is offering World Wide Web versions of 16 of its journals through a client service company in Great Britain called CatchWord, Ltd.[19] CatchWord's services are aimed at "academic publishers world-wide" (CatchWord home-page). It provides the client software, RealPage, and sets access limitations per the publisher's specifications. Handling of subscriptions, pricing, and licensing are still up to the publisher to determine.

CONCLUSION

The growth of network access to serials and articles is expanding as providers of scholarly material experiment with new relationships involving scholarly societies, commercial publishers, technology providers, and libraries. Commercial publishers are testing the marketplace and experimenting with delivery methods. Standards such as HTML and delivery technology are constantly undergoing change. Network based publishing is not a static environment.

As noted above some libraries have been active collaborators in testing user interfaces, providing indexing for searching, text processing and archiving. Librarians have the opportunity to be involved in developing criteria for evaluating these new services, even in a changing environment. Such criteria include the impact on the end user in terms of on-screen display, printing, navigation, scholarly dependability and peer review, and access to other databases, and documents. The criteria can be extended to evaluating the usefulness of licensing agreements in meeting user needs and in preserving the scholarly record. These new arrangements also call for librarians to evaluate the role of local library bibliographic databases in providing description, access, and links to these new products.

NOTES

1. There are a number of commercial publishers offering popular or non-peer reviewed serials on the World Wide Web, which are full or partial versions of print serials. Some of these include The CMP Technology Database, which provides editorial content from many of its publications and Ziff-Davis. The publisher of *Omni,* a popular press publication, converted from print to World Wide Web publishing exclusively in 1995. According to one estimate, there are, as of March 1996, approximately 175 online newspapers available on the World Wide Web (William Casey, *Washington Post,* Mar. 11, 1996, Washington Business section, 20). Many of these provide partial content from the print versions.

2. F. W. Lancaster, "The Evolution of Electronic Publishing," *Library Trends* 43, no. 4 (spring 1995): 518-27. See also: Linda Langschied, "The Changing Shape of the Electronic Journal," *Serials Review* 17, No. 3 (Fall 1991): 7-14; Ann B. Piternick, "Attempts to Find Alternatives to the Scientific Journal: a Brief Review," *The Journal of Academic Librarianship* 15, no. 5 (Nov. 1989): 260-66.

3. Cliff McKnight, "Electronic Journals–Past, Present . . . and Future?" *Aslib Proceedings* 45, no. 1 (Jan. 1993): 7.

4. Ann Okerson, "The Electronic Journal: What, Whence, and When?" The *Public-Access Computer Systems Review* 2, no. 1 (1991): 12. Available from: gopher://info.lib.uh.edu:70/00/articles/e-journals/uhlibrary/pacsreview/v2/n1/okerson. 2n1.

5. *Astrophysical Journal Letters (ApJL).* Electronic version available from: http://supernova.aas.org/ApJ/apj.html.

6. Frank Quinn, "Roadkill on the Electronic Highway? the Threat to the Mathematical Literature," *Publishing Research Quarterly* 11, no. 2 (summer 1995): 27.

7. Gary Taubes, "Science Journals Go Wired" *Science Magazine* 271, no. 5250 (9 Feb. 1996): 767.

8. *InterJournal* home page available from: http://dynamics.bu.edu/InterJournal/interj.html

9. Project Muse home page available from: http://muse.jhu.edu.

10. Richard E. Lucier and Peter Brantley, "The Red Sage Project an Experimental Digital Journal Library for the Health Sciences" *D-Lib Magazine* (Aug. 1995) (no pagination). Available from: http://www.dlib.org/dlib/august95/08lucier.html.

11. Stuart L. Weibel, "The World Wide Web and Emerging Internet Resource Discovery Standards for Scholarly Literature," *Library Trends* 43, no. 4 (spring 1995): 630.

12. Mcknight, 9.

13. David A. Fryxell, "OCLC, Founded at the Dawn of the Digital Age," *Link-up* 13, issue 1 (Jan./Feb. 1996): 14-15.

14. Roderick D. Atkinson and Laurie E. Stackpole, "TORPEDO: Networked Access to Full-Text and Page-Image Representations of Physics Journals and Technical Reports," The *Public-Access Computer Systems Review* 6, no. 3 (1995): Available from: gopher://info.lib.uh.edu:70/00/articles/e-journals/uhlibrary/pacsreview/v6/n3/Atkinson.6n3.

15. TULIP, The University Licensing Program home page. Available from: http://www.elsevier.nl/info/projects/tulip.htm.

16. Taubes, 764.

17. Academic Press home page. Available from: http://www.hbuk.co.uk/ap/.

18. For example, non-subscribers can view a demonstration of EJTC from: http://ejtc.wiley.co.uk.

19. Taylor & Francis home page. Available from: http://www.tandf.co.uk/. CatchWord, Ltd. home page. Available from: http://129.24.201.145/realhome.htm

Electronic Murmurs
from the Desk of an Ink-Stained Wretch

Joe Morehead

> The Internet is a transformation of our world, and in the course of things it has been carelessly sanctified here and there.
>
> —James Gleick

GPO ACCESS

Our story begins (with appropriate flashbacks *infra*) June 8, 1993, with the enactment of the Government Printing Office Electronic Information Enhancement Act of 1993 (PL 103-40; 107 Stat. 112, 44 U.S.C. 4101). Pursuant to S. 564, the purpose of the statute is to "establish in the Government Printing Office [GPO] a means of enhancing electronic public access to a wide range of Federal electronic information."[1] For decades the scope of GPO's involvement in the production and dissemination of government information has been contested by executive branch agencies and private sector organizations. For starters, the GPO, an agency of the Congress, has enjoyed a dubious reputation as an inept, low-tech opera-

Joe Morehead is affiliated with the School of Information Science and Policy, State University of New York at Albany, Draper Hall 141-D, 135 Western Avenue, Albany, NY 12222.

[Haworth co-indexing entry note]: "Electronic Murmurs from the Desk of an Ink-Stained Wretch." Morehead, Joe. Co-published simultaneously in *The Serials Librarian* (The Haworth Press, Inc.) Vol. 29, No. 3/4, 1996, pp. 33-46; and: *Serials Management in the Electronic Era: Papers in Honor of Peter Gellatly, Founding Editor of* The Serials Librarian (ed: Jim Cole, and James W. Williams) The Haworth Press, Inc., 1996, pp. 33-46. Single or multiple copies of this article are available for a fee from The Haworth Document Delivery Service [1-800-342-9678, 9:00 a.m. - 5:00 p.m. (EST). E-mail address: getinfo@ haworth.com].

tion. A plan "for a centralized, one-stop shopping program for online access to federal information resources . . . concerned which agency would provide such a service." The National Technical Information Service (NTIS), an entity within the Commerce Department, was a leading candidate for the job. There was also talk of creating "an entirely new federal agency or government sponsored enterprise (GSE) to provide this service."[2]

Furthermore, there exists a constitutional unease concerning GPO's domain, especially the publications of executive branch units. President Clinton gave voice to this perennial issue when he signed the Legislative Branch Appropriations Act of 1995 (PL 103-283, July 22, 1994). He noted that the Act "raises serious constitutional concerns by requiring that executive branch agencies receive a certification from the Public Printer [who as the head of the GPO is a presidential appointment, with the Senate's consent] before procuring the production of certain Government documents outside of the Government Printing office. In addition, the Act expands the types of material that are to be produced by the Government Printing Office beyond that commonly recognized as 'printing.'" Clinton thus asserted that he would "interpret the amendments to the public printing provisions in a manner that minimizes the potential constitutional deficiencies in the Act."[3]

Nevertheless, when GPO got the nod for the task of supplying the public with online information for all the branches of the federal establishment, the opposition won some small victories. In the report of the Committee on House Administration, it was noted "that nothing in the bill authorizes the Superintendent of Documents to impose conditions or requirements on the creation, dissemination, redissemination, use or reuse of Federal electronic information or electronic directories by Federal agencies or the public."[4]

In James Love's lively account of the politics involved in this fracas, a process that he traces back to 1989, the American Library Association backed a vitiated version of the measure that eventually became the Act of 1993 because of its concern "that attempts to hold out for a stronger bill would lead to lengthy delays, and possibly renewed attempts to NTIS or data vendors to further weaken or defeat the legislation." Therefore, whereas "the legislation might have been a stronger statement regarding the need for an integrated government-wide online service, GPO nevertheless had finally obtained a clear statutory mandate to provide online access to federal information." GPO's success, Love avers, will depend on its technical savvy and the cooperation of the executive branch agencies.[5]

GPO's answer to critics who have questioned its technical proficiency, notably the General Accounting Office in its report *Government Printing Office: Monopoly-Like Status Contributes to Inefficiency and Ineffectiveness* (GAO/GGD-90-107, September 26, 1990), was a 1991 tract in which the agency posed a rhetorical question: "Does GPO have a future?" The answer, some forty pages later, was a resounding affirmation; its future will be "vibrant and exciting." The bright vision involved an expansion of GPO's electronic product and service capabilities and a change in structure "from a function-based organization to a flexible, customer-based organization."[6] As for executive branch cooperation, it is interesting to note that the American Library Association, commenting on a 1979 bill that would have removed GPO from congressional jurisdiction, said "We support the creation of the Government Printing Office as an independent establishment of the Executive Branch to provide printing and distribution services for all branches of government."[7] The "constitutional" issue Clinton raised, concerning what instrumentality of the national government can best disseminate information, is merely the latest salvo in a skirmish that has never been resolved. It is, at bottom, a political issue involving matters of turf and power between the executive and legislative arms of government.

PROVISIONS

Unlike many laws, the Act of 1993 is quite the opposite of a sufflated directive. Its pith permits easy synopsis. Under the Act the Superintendent of Documents is required to maintain an electronic directory of federal electronic information (known as the Locator Service); provide a system of online access to the *Congressional Record*, the *Federal Register*, and "other appropriate publications distributed by the Superintendent of Documents"; and operate an electronic storage facility for federal information (the Storage Facility).[8] A fourth feature, called the Federal Bulletin Board, permits such amenities as online ordering of sales publications, instant retrieval of new product announcements, and "free and low cost information on demand from over 25 Federal agencies and organizations."[9] The four components together constitute what the agency has dubbed "GPO Access," and its most attractive feature is entry to that pullulating organism called the Internet.

GATEWAYS

Gateways to GPO Access began as a project in which a "participating depository library can extend no-fee, off-site public access to GPO's online services, through the library's own computer resources or an arrangement with a state or local public network." It enables you or me to "connect from home or office to the GPO Access databases . . . without charge."[10] According to a note in the quarterly *Documents to the People*, "the first functioning Gateway was a collaboration between the Columbia Online Information Network (COIN) and the University of Missouri at Columbia." Some "positive outcomes" from this Gateway initiative: "expanded exposure" to government information; lower costs for GPO to maintain the system; an incremental increase in the number of sources available on the system.[11] Remember, the law mentions only the *Congressional Record* and the *Federal Register*, but permits other publications "as determined by the Superintendent of Documents" to be added to the data bank.[12] Perhaps we have become blasé about rapid advancement in electronic communications, but it is astonishing to ponder the fact that since October 1994 anyone with a PC, modem and communications software can access a growing body of useful government information twenty-four hours a day, seven days a week.

GPO's stated goal "is to have at least one gateway library in every state," and as of May 1995 "over 85 depositories approached GPO expressing interest in becoming 'Model Gateway Libraries' to offer the use of GPO Access to remote public users."[13] In the June 15, 1995 issue of *Administrative Notes*, fifteen gateways were listed, the majority accessible via telnet, more recent volunteers via the World Wide Web.[14] For snail mail devotees, issues of the monthly *Administrative Notes*, the official newsletter of the Library Programs Service, Superintendent of Documents, Government Printing Office, provide accurate information on this initiative and many other matters affecting government publications generally and federal depository libraries in particular. For the most impatient among us, a faster way of obtaining current information on GPO Access' expanding empire (Kipling would have penned a poem in praise of GPO Access by now) is available through a service called "U.S. Fax Watch." To request copies of U.S.F.W., dial (202) 512-1716, press 4 and press 4 again; you will then be prompted to enter certain numbers (below) and your fax phone number. For this expenditure of energy, you'll receive any of four documents, as follows:

Number	*Contents and Number of Pages*
3352	The Gateway Program and General Background (10 p.)
3353	Frequently Asked Questions (8 p.)
3354	Gateway Connections and Contacts (7 p.)
3357	Registration; Selective Housing; SWAIS or WAIS? (11 p.)

These documents provide the "ground rules of the Gateway Program, copies of the fax-in registration form, the model selective agreement for electronic resources, a listing of all gateway sites," and related news and information.[15]

HOME PAGE

Like every other individual or institution in the observable universe, it seems, GPO established its own Web page, providing a starting point and a roadmap for finding information published by the federal establishment. Included are the bulletin board, online, and locator services mentioned earlier in this account; information about sales publications; the names and addresses of U.S. Government Bookstores throughout the country; and a component called "GPO On-Demand Delivery Services." This last feature permits the user to view and download Adobe Acrobat files from selected

CD-ROMs and the several GPO databases. As products and services expand, the Home Page, of course, will reflect the proliferating contents. The Universal Resource Locator (URL) for this Web address:[16] http://www.access.gpo.gov/su_docs/

SERIALS

It is tempting, and not altogether extravagant, to proclaim that the vast majority of federal government serials, series, and sets, which constitute about eighty percent of the total, are or soon will be available in an electronic format of one sort or another. To provide a laundry list of what now exists via GPO Access, much less what is to come, would surely be an exercise in futility and fatuity. Having said that, a minuscule, selective chronicle of the earliest specified serials, compiled in the summer of 1995, can be applied synecdochically. In the brief list that follows I have supplied the Superintendent of Documents classification notation and the Depository Item Number for the equivalent *print* edition of these electronically accessible sources.[17] Most of the series below are issued in paper copy; those provided in microfiche only are designated by the symbol MF. Moreover, FT in an entry indicates full text; its absence signifies a source that provides only bibliographic information.

Congressional Record [X 1.1/a; 994-B; FT: daily][18]

Federal Register [AE 2.106; 573-C; FT: daily]

Congressional Bills [Senate: Y 1.4/1; 1006-A; FT; MF: irregular]

           [House: Y 1.4/6; 1006-A; FT; MF: irregular]

United States Code [Y 1.2/5; 991-A; FT: annual supplements]

GAO Reports and Testimony [GA 1.16/3; 546-E; FT: irregular]

Monthly Catalog of United States Government Publications [GP 3.8: 557-A]

Budget of the United States Government [PREX 2.8; 853; FT: annual]

Economic Report of the President [PR 4_.9; 848; FT: annual]

Consumer Information Catalog [GS 11.9; 580-B: quarterly]

List of Classes of United States Government Publications Available for Selection by Depository Libraries [GP 3.24; 556-C: quarterly]

Add to the above, important and useful sources such as the Department of the Army's Country Studies series[19] and several sequences issued by the various geographical divisions of the State Department, which involve different SuDocs and depository item numbers; further add the numerous serials generated by other departments and agencies of the executive branch; and the potential magnitude of electronic availability becomes manifest. Concerning federal serials, six titles, all depository items, were included in a list of "Top 100 serials" announced in the *OCLC Newsletter* of January/February 1995. The list was based upon the "number of library holdings symbols attached to the cataloging records for the various titles." In descending order of "popularity," the serials are:

Statistical Abstract of the United States [C 3.134; 150: annual]

United States Government Manual [AE 2.108/2; 577: annual]

Monthly Labor Review [L 2.6; 770]

FDA Consumer [HE 20.4010; 475-H; issued ten times a year]

Occupational Outlook Handbook [L 2.3/4; 768-C-2; biennial]

County and City Data Book [C 3.134/2:C 83/2; 151: irregular][20]

The landmark Printing Act of 1895 (28 Stat. 601) established the office of Superintendent of Documents and refined the distribution of printed government documents to the 420 depository libraries then designated by the Congress. Today we have some 1400 depository institutions, and materials are shipped in print, on microfiche, on CD-ROMs, and now in the ether. On March 26, 1895, the Public Printer, Thomas Benedict, appointed Mr. F. A. Crandall of Buffalo, New York, as the first Superintendent of Documents in our nation's history. I wonder what he would think of the Federal Depository Library Program (FDLP) today?

WHAT'S IT ALL ABOUT, ALGAE?[21]

Perhaps the most fascinating development in computer technology goes far beyond the present unstructured status of the Internet; it involves a merger of computers and biology. We have known for over two decades the feasibility of designing on computers "the genes for organic molecules that never have existed previously in nature." Conversely, "gene-splicing technology eventually might create microorganisms capable of producing highly miniaturized microprocessors constructed out of organic molecules. If a gene could be designed that specified for molecular electronic circuits, thousands of infinitesimally tiny computers could be fermented out of vats of bacteria. . . . Such computers would be capable of extremely rapid calculations, since the speed at which a computer works is largely determined by the distance that signals must travel through its circuits."[22]

The human brain consists of organic molecules that combine to form a highly sophisticated network of switches, like a parallel-processing computer but one that can think, feel, perceive, and manipulate. Scientists believe they "can exploit some special properties of biological molecules–particularly proteins–to build computer components that are smaller, faster and more powerful than any electronic devices on the drawing boards thus far." This "hybrid technology," a combination of molecules and semiconductors, "should provide computers that are one-fiftieth the size and as much as 100 times faster than current ones."[23]

According to Oxford University biologist Richard Dawkins, "What is truly revolutionary about molecular biology . . . is that it has become digital. . . . After Watson and Crick, we know that genes themselves, within their minute internal structure, are long strings of pure digital information. What is more, they are truly digital, in the full and strong sense of computers and compact disks, not in the weak sense of the nervous system. The genetic code is not a binary code as in computers . . . but a quaternary code, with four symbols. The machine code of the genes is uncannily computerlike. Apart from differences in jargon, the pages of a molecular biology journal might be interchanged with those of a computer-engineering journal."[24] Indeed, computer analogies abound in the current natural science literature. For example, proteins bend DNA to their bidding, and the double helix becomes a kind of "transportation device to get two proteins together. It's like a floppy disk for a computer. . . . Normally, the floppy disk, the DNA, feeds instructions to the computer–it's the software of the cell."[25]

The congruence between the computer and biological processes raises the interesting notion that all of human mental life is ultimately physical. That the brain is reducible to a biological computer is a cornerstone of the new materialism. A major problem, however, with this mechanistic view of life is why consciousness exists at all and why subjective experience, which largely gives life its meaning, ever arose in evolution. The burgeoning discipline of evolutionary psychology attempts, within the framework of the neo-Darwinian paradigm, to answer these kinds of basic questions.[26] Dawkins is quite convinced that this digital revolution at the very core of life has dealt the *coup de grâce* to the philosophy of vitalism. "What lies at the heart of every living thing is not some sort of Bergsonian élan vital; it is information, words, instructions. . . . If you want a metaphor, if you want to understand life, think about information technology."[27]

Thus, when Robert R. Birge in the March 1995 issue of *Scientific American* writes about a "hybrid computer" that "can be designed to function as a neural associative computer capable of learning and of analyzing data and images in much the same way as the human brain," he is not talking science fiction.[28] That the information technology of the genes is digital is irrefutable reality, and the fact that DNA is a quaternary alphabet is minor. "There is very little difference, in principle, between a two-state binary information technology like ours, and a four-state information technology like that of the living cell."[29] The implications not only for artificial intelligence but also for religion and philosophy are profound.

Those of us who lay no claim to scientific literacy can sit on the sidelines and see how this glorious entertainment will play out, while keeping in mind the words of James D. Watson, co-discoverer with Francis H. C. Crick of the structure of DNA:

> One could not be a successful scientist without realizing that, in contrast to the popular conception supported by newspapers and mothers of scientists, a goodly number of scientists are not only narrow-minded and dull, but also just stupid.[30]

A GRAND VISION OR A GREAT CONFUSION

GPO Access is but a minuscule part of the misnamed "information superhighway." According to a January 1995 analysis by the General Accounting Office (GAO), policy makers and public interest groups are beginning to form a common vision of the highway's capabilities. There is an emerging agreement that it should be structured as a metanetwork that will seamlessly link thousands of broadband digital networks; allow a two-way flow of information, where users can both receive and transmit large volumes of digital data; be open, permitting equal access for service and network providers; ensure the security and privacy of databases and users' communications; and provide a high degree of interoperability and reliability.[31]

The superhighway is in its infancy, of course. Interconnected computer systems are vulnerable to attacks, often by teen-age hackers simply out to prove their ingenuity. Worms and Trojan Horse programs have from time to time damaged or compromised data and denied service to thousands of workers at the nation's major research centers. Achieving interoperability, defined as the ability of two or more components of a system or network to interact in a meaningful way, will be difficult. Reliability is essential as the public and private sectors become increasingly dependent on telecommunications networks.[32]

Equal access to the Internet and its alpha daughter the World Wide Web raises the perennial issue of the information rich/information poor dichotomy. While many can easily afford one or more of the online servicers such as Prodigy, CompuServe, America Online, E-World, or Microsoft Network, with their rich array of information abetted by Web browsers like Netscape, Spyglass, and Internet Explorer, the vast majority of Americans don't even have a home computer and fewer still own modems. The GAO study, while cautiously optimistic, does not gloss over the problems: "The telecommunications industry is deploying, or plans to deploy, a host of technologies and services that are based on ill-defined, anticipatory, or competing standards. A coordinated approach will help reduce the risk of the superhighway being fragmented into thousands of poorly integrated networks providing a bewildering choice of incompatible services." Despite the caveats, the report avers that with "effective cooperation" between "major public and private players," the "promise of the information superhighway can be attained."[33]

POLLYANNA vs. CASSANDRA

Nicholas Negroponte, founding director of the Massachusetts Institute of Technology's avant-garde Media Lab, envisages a future in which we will all have private multimedia "butlers" programmed by voice command to screen our telephone calls, schedule our days, and select our entertainment. Americans will spend more time on the Internet than on mingling with other people. Video-on-demand will have put videocassette rental stores like Blockbuster out of business. The bits of information that stream into our living rooms will be converted into customized newspapers. Raw data about the weather or about a football game will be converted at our discretion into a printout chart, a verbal report, a video picture, or a miniature re-creation. The world will be decentralized, globalized, harmonized, and people will be empowered and live happily ever after.[34]

On the other hand, Clifford Stoll, an astronomer who penetrated and exposed a German spy ring on the Internet, is as gloomy as Negroponte is optimistic. He is also a champion of our profession. As experts in cataloging systems, librarians have "centuries of experience in dealing with books about weird topics. So answer me this: how come they're not consulted right in the beginning of the design of more databases?" Why indeed? Stoll in another passage comments on something every librarian will attest. "As computers invade libraries, librarians spend a lot of time learning how to operate them. Next time you need your library card renewed and you wonder where the librarian is hiding, check to see if he's (sic) taking a class in how to access some database."[35] Aside from Stoll's confusing clerical and professional tasks, his point may strike a responsive chord. Mainly he is ambivalent about computers: a kind of love-hate relationship emerges in his book. "Computer networks return answers–often the right ones–but they emphasize the product over the process. When I'm online, I sense the vast ocean of information available to me. But I'm alone, without a tutor or librarian."[36] The Internet is spectacularly disorganized, and it needs the mediating influence of the trained professional who is capable of imposing a bibliographic structure on the information available in cyberspace. As Jonathan Franzen asserted, "The apparent democracy of today's digital networks is an artifact of their infancy. Sooner or later, all social organisms move from anarchy toward hierarchy, and whatever order emerges from the primordial chaos of the Internet seems as likely to be dystopian as utopian."[37]

TAKING TIME TO READ

Donald S. Lamm, the chairman of W. W. Norton & Company, is skeptical about the joy that Negroponte predicts for coming generations as they embrace the electronic global information resource wrought by physics, mathematics, and biology. Noting that Negroponte forthrightly identifies himself as "someone who does not like to read," Lamm wonders if indeed the electronic revolution is going to be so stimulating that it will overcome what is referred to as *aliteracy*, defined as "the ability to read without the desire to do so." Even though the hour for the book may be late, it "will coexist with the computer, as it has had to coexist since far earlier in this century with movies and then television. Like symphony orchestras, however, books seem destined to move gradually–not today and not tomorrow–to the fringes of our culture. Their utility will not come to an end, even if books serve future generations mainly as beacons to the headlands of civilization."[38] This dirge is a dire prediction and one that I hope will not come to pass. History and experience suggest that things are never quite as bad or quite as good as the haruspices of any epoch presage. Neither a Pollyanna nor a Cassandra be: a maxim in which I have always placed my trust.

REFERENCES

1. Government Printing Office Electronic Information Access Enhancement Act of 1993, 107 Stat. 112 (June 8, 1993).

2. James P. Love, "A Window on the Politics of the Government Printing Office Electronic Information Access Enhancement Act of 1993," 21 *Journal of Government Information* 3, 5 (1994).

3. Weekly Compilation of Presidential Documents, July 29, 1994, p. 1542.

4. House Report 103-108, May 25, 1993, p. 6.

5. Love, p. 12.

6. *Strategic Planning, GPO/2001: Vision for a New Millennium* (Washington, DC: Government Printing Office, December 1991), pp. iii, 15, 22 et seq.

7. U.S. Congress. House, Committee on House Administration, and Senate, Committee on Rules and Administration, *Public Printing Reorganization Act of 1979, Hearings*, 96th Cong., 1st Sess., July 10, 19, 24, 26, 1979, p. 126.

8. Ibid., supra, note 1.

9. See 16 *Administrative Notes* 2-3 (January 15, 1995); 16 *Administrative Notes* 11 (July 15, 1995).

10. 16 *Administrative Notes* 3 (January 15, 1995).

11. Maurie Caitlin Kelly, "GPO Access Initiative," 22 *Documents to the People* 255 (December 1994).

12. Ibid., supra, note 1.

13. 16 *Administrative Notes* 7 (May 15, 1995).

14. 16 *Administrative Notes* 6-9 (June 15, 1995).

15. Ibid., p. 5.

16. 16 *Administrative Notes* 11 (July 15, 1995).

17. Based on current information in the *List of Classes of United States Government Publications Available for Selection by Depository Libraries* (GP 3.24; 556-C). The *List of Classes* is revised quarterly in print but its electronic version is updated monthly in ACSII format and located on the Federal Bulletin Board.

18. GPO's four aging web letterpresses were phased out in the summer of 1995 and replaced by three new offset presses. The latter permit an improvement in print quality and in the ability to utilize recycled newsprint for the printing of the *Congressional Record* and the *Federal Register*. (19 *Newsletter, United States Government Printing Office* 1 (June/July 1995).

19. The Country Studies, formerly called the Army Area Handbooks, are issued within the Department of the Army Pamphlet 500 series (D 101.22; 327-J).

20. 16 *Administrative Notes* 15 (June 15, 1995).

21. Protists are the unicellular prototype of all subsequent plant and animal life, including *Homo sapiens sapiens*. They were the first microscopic beings with nuclei and include the eukaryotic algae. This fact tickled my memory, and an abnormal gene has predisposed me to pun the title of this section on the name of the theme song of the classic 1966 movie *Alfie*.

22. Christopher Lampton, *DNA and the Creation of New Life* (NY: Arco, 1983), pp. 113-14.

23. Robert R. Birge, "Protein-Based Computers," *Scientific American*, March 1995, p. 90. Birge is professor of chemistry, director of the W. M. Keck Center for Molecular Electronics, and research director of the New York State Center for Advanced Technology in Computer Applications and Software Engineering at Syracuse University.

24. Richard Dawkins, *River Out of Eden: A Darwinian View of Life* (NY: Basic Books, 1995), pp. 16-17. DNA, deoxyribonucleic acid, a double-stranded, long-

chain molecule in which the two strands are twisted into the famous double helix, flows through time. "It is a river of information . . . a river of abstract instructions for building bodies." (p. 4).

25. Natalie Angier, *The Beauty of the Beastly: New Views on the Nature of Life* (Boston: Houghton Mifflin, 1995), p. 81. See also her Chapter 15, "DNA's Unbroken Text," pp. 89-94, which extends the computer metaphor.

26. For a useful discussion of this phenomenon, see Robert Wright, *The Moral Animal* (NY: Pantheon, 1994), Chapter 17, pp. 345-63.

27. Richard Dawkins, *The Blind Watchmaker* (NY: Norton, 1986), p. 112.

28. Birge, p. 95.

29. Dawkins, *The Blind Watchmaker*, p. 114. See also Chapter 5, "The Power and the Archives," pp. 111-37 for an expansion of this fundamental notion.

30. James D. Watson, *The Double Helix* (NY: Atheneum, 1968), p. 14.

31. U.S. General Accounting Office. *Information Superhighway: An Overview of Technology Challenges*, January 1995 (GAO/AIMD-95-23), p. 11.

32. Ibid., pp. 19, 31-33, 35-40.

33. Ibid, p. 41.

34. Nicholas Negroponte, *Being Digital* (NY: Knopf, 1995), passim.

35. Clifford Stoll, *Silicon Snake Oil: Second Thoughts on the Information Highway* (NY: Doubleday, 1995), pp. 211-12.

36. Ibid., p. 124.

37. In a review of *Being Digital* in *The New Yorker*, March 7, 1995, p. 119.

38. Donald S. Lamm, "Life Outside Academe," 60 *The Key Reporter* 6-7 (Summer 1995).

The Significance
of Information Provision and Content:
Libraries as Information Providers
Instead of Format Collectors

Elizabeth (Libby) Cooley
Edward A. Goedeken

SUMMARY. The significance of information, the way it is provided, and the impact of its format are addressed. The advent of the electronic format has required libraries to regard themselves as information providers instead of format collectors. This analysis discusses how the issue of providing information transcends the traditional task of collecting it within an environment based on a work-oriented approach. The authors show that the quickest and most efficient way to incorporate provision and content is by using previously established practice and *refining* it to work with unfamiliar formats. *[Article copies available for a fee from The Haworth Document Delivery Service: 1-800-342-9678. E-mail address: getinfo@haworth.com]*

INTRODUCTION

The Information Revolution of the past several decades has spurred the library community to address a wide range of issues

---

Elizabeth (Libby) Cooley is Biotechnology Bibliographer, and Edward Goedeken is Principal Humanities Bibliographer at the Parks Library, Iowa State University, Ames, IA 50011-2140.

[Haworth co-indexing entry note]: "The Significance of Information Provision and Content: Libraries as Information Providers Instead of Format Collectors." Cooley, Elizabeth (Libby), and Edward A. Goedeken. Co-published simultaneously in *The Serials Librarian* (The Haworth Press, Inc.) Vol. 29, No. 3/4, 1996, pp. 47-56; and: *Serials Management in the Electronic Era: Papers in Honor of Peter Gellatly, Founding Editor of* The Serials Librarian (ed: Jim Cole, and James W. Williams) The Haworth Press, Inc., 1996, pp. 47-56. Single or multiple copies of this article are available for a fee from The Haworth Document Delivery Service [1-800-342-9678, 9:00 a.m. - 5:00 p.m. (EST). E-mail address: getinfo@haworth.com].

relating to providing and collecting information for patron use. The centuries-old environment of print has been shaken by the advent of the electronic medium, which has added a new dimension to the library's central cultural role of managing a society's production of information. In this analysis we will show how the issue of providing information transcends the traditional task of collecting it within an environment based on a work-oriented approach, which is defined by David Levy and Catherine Marshall as the following: "By a work-oriented approach to digital libraries, we do not mean an approach that focuses solely on people's work, but rather one that evaluates library collections and technology in relation to the work that is being done with them."[1] It is this focus on how information is used–instead of the traditional approach of collecting it to perform the role of an "archival storehouse"–that is crucial to why libraries need to shift their focus, in a work-oriented environment, from the passive act of collecting to the active process of providing information to the user.

INFORMATION VERSUS FORMAT

In carrying out a work-oriented approach to the functions of information, one needs to investigate what is being provided: information or format. In other words, do libraries serve as a dynamic means for access to information, or do they serve as secure repositories for packaged data? Perhaps because of the newness of the electronic environment, many professionals have gotten into the habit of looking at format first, instead of the information it contains. It is easy to assume that all information in the future will be in an electronic format, but like many visions, in reality this is fantasy. As Clifford Stoll states:

> One of the great promises of the online world is fast access to great quantities of information. Internet proponents talk of libraries without books, the time when essentially all publications will be available over the network. We'll be able to read and access any document from our workstations. Books will be distributed electronically. I claim that this bookless library

is a dream, a hallucination of online addicts, network neo-phytes, and library-automation insiders.[2]

Clifford Lynch professes that this sentiment is also true within the library community:

> The paperless world envisioned by some futurists over the recent decades has little credibility with most of the academic publishing and library communities. A central question bearing on the rate at which transition to electronic collections and electronic publishing will proceed is the extent to which new information technology innovations can supplant largely paper-based technology and, if they only supplement rather than replace the present environment, whether they will return the predicted economic benefits.[3]

PROVIDING VERSUS COLLECTING

Many professionals have become so consumed by this online environment that they have forgotten to look at the information itself first before deciding the most appropriate format. These same professionals tend to focus on the collection of, rather than the provision of, information. At the other extreme, an electronic environment has frightened many professionals into an endless round of task forces and committees to determine how best to cope with this new format, often resulting in an extended delay to users in the provision of information. Jean-Claude Guedon correctly observes that:

> Librarians, for their part, have eyed the advent of the information age with some anxiety. They realize that it promises if not to destroy print (as some have foolishly claimed), at least to relocate it in a major, even radical, fashion. As custodians of information and as professionals deeply wedded to the print form, they worry about the ways in which a shift away from this tried and trusted medium is going to affect their work habits, the value of their skills and, ultimately, their professional status.[4]

Being "wedded to the print form" forces librarians to focus on format and how it will be assimilated into an existing, largely print-based, collection. A middle ground concerning selection must be reached which selects information first, regardless of format, after which it concerns itself with the most appropriate format, and then quickly makes it all available to the patron. Mistakes may be made during the early stages of this process, but the user benefits from quicker access to information regardless of the format. Provision and content should outweigh questions of collecting and format. To this end Erwin Welsch assures us that:

> This is where librarians should find their niche: identifying resources regardless of format and encouraging suppliers of network information to make their products readily and easily available. Focusing their future role not on being a warehouse of electronic or printed information, but on becoming an information utility that locates data in diverse sources seems more appropriate. Simply duplicating the collection practices we evolved for print materials in the network environment does not seem responsive to current needs or capabilities. Given high materials costs, our current collection development practices are not even working in the print environment.[5]

Moreover, Lynch summarizes the library's traditional role as an "information utility" even more succinctly: "Libraries are organizations that carry out the functions of selecting, organizing, preserving, and providing access to information. Libraries *are not* their collections."[6] Librarians must constantly remind themselves that libraries are more than their collections, that they are fundamentally in the business of providing information in whatever format best suits the user's needs. The ranking and accrediting of a research library based on the number of volumes in its collection should be rethought because of the new reality of information provision. The concept of how a library is evaluated must be changed now that information transcends a specific shelf location.

POLICIES AND PROCEDURES

The quickest and most efficient way to incorporate provision and content consists of using previously established practice and *refining* it to accommodate electronic formats with which many librarians are still unfamiliar. Levy and Marshall insist that:

> Library developments ought to be grounded in a solid understanding of past and present practices. Without this, we risk losing still relevant structures and practices while maintaining an allegiance to mythical and irrelevant features of an unrealized past or an idealized present.[7]

One of the most vexing problems in selecting, processing and disseminating electronic information may be the existing belief in departmental territoriality which inhibits communication among the various library departments involved. This can be improved through a concerted effort to eliminate turf battles over projects and work assignments. The days of delineating clear areas of bibliographic responsibility are disappearing as libraries move into an electronic era where everyone shares the same record and uses different parts to assist the patron. Internecine struggles over the control of information within the political structure of the library environment are counterproductive to its historic mission objective of providing information to the public.

Uneasiness with electronic formats has often resulted in lengthy debates over the creation of policies and procedures for handling electronic resources within an existing structure for the selecting, processing and dissemination of information. Policies are, of course, still necessary for a smoothly operating library, as Craig Summerhill notes: "The advent of networked resources does not eliminate the need for a formal policy governing the acquisition of electronic resources."[8] But, it is *not* essential that these formal policies be in place before information is provided to the public. It must be remembered that in the past libraries struggled to compose collection development policies, yet all work did not come to a halt while this was being accomplished. Reasons often mentioned for having in place a policy prior to selecting electronic resources include concerns about how readily available the product is, as well as cost, and issues relating to acquisition and service. And though legitimate, these questions differ little from those that have always confronted the selection of print materials. F. W. Lancaster, who has written extensively on the impact of electronic resources, maintains that:

> Electronic resources present problems–problems of integrating them with more traditional forms, problems of costs of acquisition versus access, and the most critical problem of determining what "collection development" really means in an electronic environment. The role of collection development in dealing with distributed electronic sources may be little different from the print-on-paper world.[9]

For this reason, libraries should pursue a work-oriented approach to providing resources, in any format, *before* a policy is written. Since the basic procedures are similar, it is essential that they look to their existing policies and use those to govern purchases. The collection development policies should be refined throughout the process and revised to include electronic resources.

Cost reduction is often cited as a happy consequence of acquiring forthcoming information in electronic resources. Yet publishers, being for-profit organizations, will continue to focus on their profit margins, and therefore libraries should not expect to see a decrease in prices for information in electronic formats in the short term.

Serials are an excellent example of how information will continue to appear in several formats. As they adjust to producing information in multiple formats, some publishers have inadvertently delayed the distribution of the electronic version while they generate the more labor-intensive and time-consuming paper product. Once publishers become more comfortable with balancing the two formats libraries will continue acquiring some publications in the traditional paper format, while purchasing other more time-sensitive literature only in the electronic version. George Jaramillo attests to this possibility:

> Thus, the possibility exists that subscribing to a comprehensive collection of journals in a given field will no longer be as important as is so now. If journals continue to exist in printed

form, it is likely that only core items will be subscribed to in this form.[10]

STATUS ANGST

How will this affect current staffing arrangements or the professional responsibilities of library staff? Just as various units within the library have for many years used the same online catalog record, the certainty of acquiring more and more information in electronic form will only serve to encourage this steady withering away of decades-old divisions within the library. Thus, for example, technical services, reference, and collection development departments will steadily merge their work flows, a process that is already underway in many libraries. This will result in an increasing emphasis on the professional who is well versed in selecting, processing and disseminating information within the structure of the library. Jutta Reed-Scott emphasizes this point vis-à-vis collection development: "Providing access to an expanding array of information resources requires collection development librarians to have the technical knowledge to manage collections in a variety of electronic formats."[11] The traditional hierarchical nature of library organization will also be transformed to accommodate a more *team-oriented* approach to managing information within the library. The benefits of a nimbler organization will quickly become apparent to the user, who often has limited patience with the often unwieldy library bureaucracy.

FUTURE DIRECTIONS

The future for the peaceful coexistence of electronic, print and other types of information formats appears to be more secure than perhaps previously thought. It must be remembered that the advent of the telephone did not doom the writing and sending of letters, as the invention of television did not lead to the extinction of radio. Different media can exist side by side. While its packaging may certainly change, information will continue to exist in a multi-formatted environment, including formats as yet foreseen. Levy and Marshall predict that:

> We are then left with two possible futures. One is that digital-only libraries and nondigital libraries will coexist. The other is that libraries will contain digital *and* nondigital material–in which case "digital library" is a misnomer, and certainly not synonymous with "the library of the future." But the better word for these evolving institutions is "libraries," not "digital libraries," for ultimately what must be preserved is the heterogeneity of materials and practices.[12]

In this "library of the future," which many have called the "library without walls," we see another dimension closer to the hearts of library professionals: a library without staffing walls, or, in other words, a library organization that is flatter, which requires professionals with multi-dimensional skills that transcend traditional technical and public services divisions so that information can move more smoothly throughout the library organization to the benefit of the patron, whose information needs, after all, libraries are trying to serve. Communication between all library departments vis-à-vis information resources must be nurtured since the decisions as to the format in which information is acquired will impact how it is accessed and disseminated. Libraries are fully functioning, living information providers with all components playing a vital part. As Jaramillo states:

> Yet the view that libraries will become obsolete or at best archival storehouses and that librarians will become mere information consultants seems radical, and gives little credence to human nature.[13]

CONCLUSION

For libraries to function effectively and efficiently now and in the future, they need to move beyond their historical emphasis on reacting to how resources are packaged and recognize their obligation to the user to select, acquire, organize, and make available information in a timely fashion regardless of format. They need to undertake the active role of providing information, and move away from the passive task of simply collecting materials for their shelves. In order to do this librarians must also recognize that the professional responsibilities of librarianship will move ever closer to a seamless whole that denies the existence of public and technical divisions of work, but reflects the integrated reality that libraries provide information in whatever format is appropriate to their users. This future library professional will require an in-depth knowledge of the broad range of information-handling activities. The digital revolution has created a dynamic that transcends the limiting features of time and space, propelling libraries beyond their present mode of operation to an unforeseen, yet challenging future.

REFERENCES

1. David M. Levy and Catherine C. Marshall, "Going Digital: A Look at Assumptions Underlying Digital Libraries," *Communications of the ACM* 38 (April 1995): 78.

2. Clifford Stoll, *Silicon Snake Oil: Second Thoughts on the Information Highway* (New York: Doubleday, 1995), p. 176.

3. Clifford Lynch, "The Development of Electronic Publishing and Digital Library Collections on the NREN," *Electronic Networking* 1 (Winter 1991): 8. More on what Lynch thinks can be found in his *Accessibility and Integrity of Networked Information* (Washington, D.C.: United States Congress, Office of Technology Assessment, 1994).

4. Jean-Claude Guedon, "Research Libraries and Electronic Scholarly Journals: Challenges or Opportunities?" *The Serials Librarian* v. 26, nos. 3/4 (1995): 3.

5. Erwin Welsch, remarks in Charles W. Bailey, Jr. and Dana Rooks, eds. "Symposium on the Role of Networked-based Electronic Resources in Scholarly Communication and Research," *The Public-Access Computer Systems Review* [serial online] v. 2, no. 2 (1991): 44. To retrieve this article, URL to http://www.lib.ncsu.edu/stacks/pacsr-v2n02.html.

6. Lynch, "Development" p. 7.

7. Levy and Marshall, "Going Digital," p. 83.

8. Craig Summerhill, remarks in Bailey and Rooks, eds. "Symposium," p. 41.

9. F. W. Lancaster, "Collection Development in the Year 2025," in Peggy Johnson and Sheila S. Intner, eds. *Recruiting, Educating, and Training Librarians for Collection Development* (Westport, CT: Greenwood Press, 1994), p. 215. For more on the impact of electronic resources on collection development, see Michael Buckland, "What Will Collection Developers Do?" *Information Technology & Libraries* 14 (September 1995): 155-59.

10. George R. Jaramillo, "Computer Technology and Its Impact on Collection Development," *Collection Management* 10, nos.1/2 (1988): 10.

11. Jutta Reed-Scott, "Information Technologies and Collection Development," *Collection Building* 9, nos. 3-4 (1989): 50.

12. Levy and Marshall, "Going Digital," p. 79.

13. George R. Jaramillo, "Computer Technology," p. 10.

Subscription or Information Agency Services in the Electronic Era

F. Dixon Brooke, Jr.

SUMMARY. The development of the Internet, electronic journals, and questions surrounding the longevity of the paper journal have led some to wonder what the role of subscription vendors will be in the future. Regardless of future changes in the variety of information and available media, the subscription or information agency's main role–helping customers efficiently identify, procure and manage a variety of information resources–will be the same, although the methods of conducting business will change and additional services will be offered. Even if information becomes more fragmented and the "journal" as we know it ceases to exist, access to articles, through Web sites, online hosts, or other means, will probably still be available on *subscription.* Moreover, providing users with coordinated, cost-effective access to quality information about serials and articles will continue to be a challenge for libraries and organizations. Therefore, the agency services of information location, order and payment consolidation, access provision and resource management will be needed more than ever. *[Article copies available for a fee from The Haworth Document Delivery Service: 1-800-342-9678. E-mail address: getinfo@haworth.com]*

The development of the Internet, electronic journals, and questions surrounding the longevity of the paper journal have led some

---

F. Dixon Brooke, Jr. is Vice President, General Manager, EBSCO Subscription Services (a part of the EBSCO Information Services Group).

[Haworth co-indexing entry note]: "Subscription or Information Agency Services in the Electronic Era." Brooke, F. Dixon, Jr. Co-published simultaneously in *The Serials Librarian* (The Haworth Press, Inc.) Vol. 29, No. 3/4, 1996, pp. 57-65; and: *Serials Management in the Electronic Era: Papers in Honor of Peter Gellatly, Founding Editor of* The Serials Librarian (ed: Jim Cole, and James W. Williams) The Haworth Press, Inc., 1996, pp. 57-65. Single or multiple copies of this article are available for a fee from The Haworth Document Delivery Service [1-800-342-9678, 9:00 a.m. - 5:00 p.m. (EST). E-mail address: getinfo@haworth.com].

to wonder what the role of subscription vendors will be in the future. Despite the changes in the variety of information and available media that have occurred over the years and will continue to occur, the subscription or information agency's main role has been and will continue to be the same. An agency's role is to help customers procure and manage a variety of information resources. And while the methods of conducting business will always change, the basic premise or mission of the agency will not.

Subscription agencies began by offering a basic form of service: consolidated ordering, invoicing and renewal of print subscriptions (and this by far represents the bulk of agency business today, even though CD-ROM subscriptions have existed for several years). As the amount of available information grew, so did the breadth of agency services. To help libraries and organizations manage proliferating information and escalating costs, agencies began to offer claiming assistance, bibliographic information, collection development/assessment assistance, and even assistance with de-selection projects.

More recently, agencies have responded to changes in information formats by offering service for CD-ROM and other electronic subscriptions and by offering document delivery services. The continuing challenge for agencies is to help libraries manage and analyze the different types of information they buy. This will require providing libraries with an overall analysis of their journal subscriptions (both electronic and print formats), database subscriptions and article purchases to help them maximize access for users and minimize costs for their institutions.

Another challenge and responsibility for agencies is to work with publishers to optimize data flow for the benefit of customers. This includes electronic order placement with publishers, faster and more accurate processing, loading and displaying dispatch data to reduce claims, adopting claims review and acknowledgment standards for more efficient claiming, loading electronic price data received from publishers, etc. The overall goal is to maintain efficient internal processes that result in better, faster service for customers at a reasonable price.

What will constantly change for libraries, publishers and vendors is the method of conducting business. This is evident when one reviews the ways in which business transactions between libraries, agencies and publishers have changed in the past, even when the media remained the same. These changes can be examined in two key areas: customer-agency communication and transactions; and agency-publisher communication and transactions.

LIBRARY-AGENCY COMMUNICATION AND TRANSACTIONS

With the advent of computers, transactions between customers and agencies evolved and became more sophisticated, even though the bulk of the transactions concerned print journal subscriptions. For example:

- Orders were first sent to agencies through paper or voice communication. When computers and automated library systems surfaced, vendors' online systems and proprietary interfaces between vendors' mainframes and customers' systems allowed for more rapid and efficient electronic order placement. Standards for purchase order transmission are being developed to make the process even more efficient and to make it easier for automated systems to communicate with vendors' main computer systems for order placement with little or no human intervention. The same developments affected the placement of renewals and claims (however, it should be noted that standards have been developed for claims transmission but not for electronic renewals).
- The availability of invoices in electronic format has increased the speed with which libraries receive information (when it is transferred over the Internet, for example, as opposed to through the mail), enhanced accuracy and speed of posting expenditures, and put more control in the library, because electronic data can be customized or manipulated by the librarian for creative and extensive analysis. The development of standards for invoice transmission has further increased the efficiency of receiving and processing the data.
- Serials management and collection analysis reports in electronic format have provided another benefit for all parties

involved by saving paper and postage in addition to offering more rapid and flexible analysis.

- Daily communication between libraries and vendors has also evolved. Many "conversations" now occur over the Internet instead of telephone lines.

AGENCY-PUBLISHER COMMUNICATION AND TRANSACTIONS

Changes in the way agencies and publishers communicate and transact business have also evolved and created additional benefits to libraries buying print subscriptions:

- Publishers can now electronically transfer delayed publication and dispatch data to agencies. When agencies offer this data in electronic format to customers, claiming efficiency is increased, and libraries, vendors and publishers save time and money by reducing unnecessary claims. It is especially helpful when the agent also offers check-in data in addition to publisher-supplied data. When this information was available only in print, a library might have missed a publisher's claiming "window" before receiving the information or might have wasted time and money claiming issues that hadn't been published yet. This also wasted the time and resources of agencies and publishers.

- Additionally, some publishers now have the ability to provide price information to agencies in electronic format. When this is received electronically it helps the agency provide customers more accurate forecasting of future prices and more accurate price quotations. Receipt of the data also has the potential to reduce the number of "billbacks" or supplemental invoices, and increases accuracy of agency databases since the manual keying of price and other data is reduced for those publishers.

- Originally, agencies sent orders to publishers in paper format, requiring the agency to manually input order data from the customer and the publishers to manually input order data from the agency. The process was not only time-consuming but also allowed the opportunity for errors in data input. Electronic order placement, which is now possible with many publishers, offers increased speed and accuracy of order placement, resulting in more accurate fulfillment and fewer problems with matching renewals. The same is true for the claiming process. Standards have been developed for claims response, which will again increase the efficiency of the claiming process for all parties.

The migration to electronic business transactions greatly increased timeliness and productivity on all sides. These methods of communication and commerce have evolved over many years, even though the commodity–the paper journal–remained somewhat the same. However, when electronic databases became available, on CD-ROM, for example, the same methods were used for the procurement of information in a new medium. They will continue to be necessary for procurement of the newest media–electronic documents and electronic journals. Libraries will still need to know what is available and how much it costs, to engage in a renewal process each year, and to coordinate and manage procurement, access and costs. The serials information services vendor will continue its role as a facilitator in this process.

SERIALS IN THE FUTURE

Currently, much discussion centers around the prospect of author and/or strictly Internet publishing, i.e., the disappearance of commercial publishing, at least in the scholarly area. While this is certainly a possibility in the distant future, it is also likely that publishers will continue to exist, whether they be commercial scholarly publishers, universities, societies, associations or groups of scientists in specific disciplines. Organized publishing provides the necessary benefits of quality control. If information continues to proliferate at its current pace, a means of identifying or defining quality information will be needed more than ever. While because of this it is likely that we will still have many publishers in the future, the available media will multiply and change. Agencies will have a role in helping libraries identify published works and available media or delivery options.

Current journal/information media or delivery options include paper, CD-ROM, microform, site licenses, full text articles available online or on CD-ROM, current awareness and abstract services, and document delivery. In the future, the following will probably be common among campuses and institutions, along with the media and delivery options mentioned above which will then be considered more traditional ones:

- Web sites–Journals accessible via World Wide Web sites will be valuable because information can be published and distributed much faster than with traditional printing, resulting in more current information. Web sites also allow the use of photos, graphics, etc., to more closely resemble print publications or at least to include the same visual data. However, there are disadvantages associated with journals on Web sites: some require individual user passwords that will be difficult for the library to administer; not all potential subscribers will have the systems with which to access the sites adequately; and connection, software and hardware problems can curtail or delay access.

- Site licenses–Locally mounted electronic journals can provide fast access when they are readily available over several terminals or a campus or corporate network. In many cases, site licensed electronic journals can also be accessed via network software that is familiar to users and can provide access for several users at once–an attractive option for high-use journals. However, local maintenance is required in loading and interfacing data with the local network software. Also, the local software might not be able to manage photos, graphics and charts or they may not be as attractive.

- Journals mounted on remote hosts or through consortia systems–This is also a good option for high-use journals. This option will offer timeliness of information, multiple access points and, in some cases, keyword searching of data. Graphics and photos may or may not be available or of good quality. Librarians also may worry about archival access to back issues.

- Online full text articles available through remote hosts–Advantages include searchability (of ASCII text articles), and instant access to and delivery of articles. Full text article access should be coordinated with journal subscriptions for optimum effectiveness. It is helpful if the host has a mechanism for analyzing which journals are most often cited in users' results lists, so licenses, Web access or other types of cost-effective subscriptions can be purchased for frequently cited journals. Customized full text databases will also be available to allow rapid, searchable access to articles from a set of journals chosen by the library.

• Current awareness and document delivery–Current awareness services will become even more essential and readily available to help librarians and users sort through the plethora of information becoming available on the Internet and elsewhere. Such services will continue to be used to supplement local collections. Document delivery might become more of a finding service, as there will always be obscure documents and Web sites, etc., that will have valuable information. Document delivery providers will be specialists at finding these quickly and getting them to users in the most effective manner.

THE ROLE OF THE AGENCY

The subscription or serial information agency will help libraries and organizations procure and manage the "collection" described above. Continued information proliferation and fragmentation does not diminish the need for agencies; it underscores the need for assistance in information location, differentiation, organization, distribution and management. Given the probable continued existence of many and varied publishers and available media, agencies will still have a key role to play, which will probably include:

• Providing consolidated ordering and payment services–even though some predict an information Utopia where authors publish their own works and everything is available instantly over the Internet, it is highly unlikely that all pertinent information will be available for free. Therefore, there will still be a need for agencies to place orders and pay publishers, whoever they may be, for customers requiring access to many materials along with efficiency and cost control.

- Providing information about journals and available media (Web site access, licensing availability, CD-ROM, print, etc.) and about electronic full text articles. This is no different than a current agency database that lists journals available for subscription and provides information about different media (print, CD-ROM, online, microfiche, etc.) along with bibliographic and subscription ordering information.
- Gathering key information about journals, Web sites, licenses and databases, such as who "publishes" them, access or subscription costs, and payment requirements. Again, this is similar to agencies' current databases that list publishing and pricing information for print journals. For hosts providing full text articles, this might include providing a list of which journals are covered and matching that list to the library's local collection. This is similar to some current agency databases which provide information about where titles are indexed.
- Helping customers analyze total subscription or serials expenditures (whether serials are available in print, through Web access or site license), full text access, current awareness and document delivery.
- Identifying customer expenditures by department, discipline, site or cost center code.
- Identifying what information is being accessed by discipline or department–just as it is now helpful to know what is being subscribed to by the main library, the engineering library and the nursing school, in the future it will be helpful to know what is being accessed or licensed by various campus libraries or departments for coordination purposes.
- Helping librarians determine the optimum formula for maximizing access and minimizing costs. If one agency is used for most subscriptions, licenses, access and document delivery services, that agency should be in a good position to help the library arrive at a precise formula for the least expensive, most efficient information provision. The library and vendor together should be able to identify: high-use or low-cost journals appropriate for subscriptions or licenses; extremely time-sensitive materials that might necessitate Web access/subscriptions; and high-cost or low-use journals that might be better

candidates for current awareness/document delivery services or full text access via online hosts. The agency's services should include ongoing analysis so the library can shift resources as needed to continue to control costs and maximize access. For example, ongoing analysis of document delivery purchases or of articles printed from an online host might indicate when it would actually be more cost effective to subscribe to a more expensive journal.

CONCLUSION

The subscription or information agency's services in the electronic era of serials will be essentially the same as they are today although the methods of conducting business will change and additional services will be offered. Even if information becomes more fragmented and the "journal" as we know it ceases to exist, access to articles, through Web sites, online hosts, or other means, will probably still be available on *subscription*. Moreover, providing users with coordinated, cost-effective access to quality information about serials and articles will continue to be a challenge for libraries and organizations, and the agency services of information location, order consolidation, access provision and resource management will be needed more than ever.

Proposals for Interinstitutional Serials Cooperation at the SUNY Centers

Suzanne Fedunok

SUMMARY. This paper discusses CLR grant-assisted projects under-taken by the four SUNY University Center Libraries regarding the issue of resource sharing of low use/high cost periodicals. Other recent consortial initiatives are mentioned. The impact of "Rethinking SUNY" is discussed. *[Article copies available for a fee from The Haworth Document Delivery Service: 1-800-342-9678. E-mail address: getinfo@haworth.com]*

The State University of New York system is made up of four doctoral granting university centers, thirteen liberal arts colleges, eight specialized colleges, four medical schools and six colleges of technology and agriculture. Each institution has a distinct mission and curricular interests and the various SUNY academic libraries reflect these differences in their collections. As part of a Council on Library Resources (CLR) grant project in 1992/93 the four doctoral-granting institutions of the State University of New York–the SUNY University Centers at Albany, Binghamton, Buffalo, and Stony Brook–conducted a comprehensive study of journal use. Journals were the focus of the study because they account for the

Suzanne Fedunok is Reference Librarian/Bibliographer at the Binghamton University Libraries–SUNY, P.O. Box 6012, Binghamton, NY 13902-6012. E-mail: sfedunok@library.lib.binghamton.edu.

[Haworth co-indexing entry note]: "Proposals for Interinstitutional Serials Cooperation at the SUNY Centers." Fedunok, Suzanne. Co-published simultaneously in *The Serials Librarian* (The Haworth Press, Inc.) Vol. 29, No. 3/4, 1996, pp. 67-77; and: *Serials Management in the Electronic Era: Papers in Honor of Peter Gellatly, Founding Editor of* The Serials Librarian (ed: Jim Cole, and James W. Williams) The Haworth Press, Inc., 1996, pp. 67-77. Single or multiple copies of this article are available for a fee from The Haworth Document Delivery Service [1-800-342-9678, 9:00 a.m. - 5:00 p.m. (EST). E-mail address: getinfo@haworth.com].

largest part of Centers' library materials expenditures; they are subject to the biggest price increases; and, with the advent of Z39.50 and the soon-to-be installed NOTIS PacLink system at three of the four campuses, they were thought to be eminently shareable.

The four university libraries were committed to move from independently designed and managed cancellation projects on the four campuses to annual collaborations. The study was designed "to determine whether there were any journal titles held by more than one of the University Center libraries which received sufficiently low use to justify retention of only one copy, which the other SUNY Centers could access via interlibrary loan and document delivery services. . . . By focussing on real needs, rather than building redundant collections, the SUNY Centers will become more responsive, more financially responsible, more manageable." [1]

The main results of the journal use study appeared in an earlier paper. [2] This paper will summarize that information and bring the picture regarding the Centers' interinstitutional serials cooperation up to date.

"Hard data" to inform library policy was one of the themes of the CLR project. As a result of the study, the SUNY University Center libraries for the first time would have hard data on the scope and use of their current and retrospective journal collections. The journal use study began with the creation of a one-time-only "snapshot" union list of the 11,000 journal titles subscribed to at the four campuses. Upon examination, this union list offered hope for cooperation, on the basis of sharing unique titles and of reducing unnecessary duplication. Over half (52%) of the journals were held at only one campus. This richness of unique holdings was something of a surprise. Many of these titles were in foreign languages and the titles were largely in the humanities and the social sciences.

A detailed study of the use of all journals, bound and unbound, on the four campuses was the next step. The instances of journal use recorded during the year were analyzed, and the results confirmed that a significant number of low-use titles might be candidates for sharing. Over one third (36%) of the journal titles–mostly uniquely held ones–had been used five or fewer times.

Another goal of the grant was to "define the specific operating policies under which cooperation can function among the SUNY

University Center Libraries." As a means to that end, four lists were produced to inform future collaborative collection management decisions:

1. low-use or no-use unique titles (56% of the unique titles had no reported use);
2. little-used duplicated titles (675 duplicated titles got five or fewer uses);
3. titles that were heavily used on one campus and little used on the others;
4. heavily used unique titles.

Based on the journal use study results, three of the four campuses promptly acted independently and "on principle" to cancel titles with no recorded use. This led to a theoretical surplus of funds, the disposition of which became an interesting object of speculation discussed below. All four campuses used the data to identify titles with high cost/low use. This cost-per-use calculation was later refined into a "cost/benefit decision rule" by another study.

As a final step in the project, the collection development officers drafted a plan called the "SUNY University Centers Cooperative Journals Program." This plan envisioned a yearly exchange of information and decision-making among the four library systems including a procedure for notification, review, and appeal of journals cancellations and acquisitions plans and the implementation of agreements and procedures for rapid document delivery from the Centers' collections.

The four libraries agreed on the following criteria to be used for collaborative serials decisions:

- level of use;
- cost per use;
- holdings of titles among participating libraries;
- demand for new titles;
- availability of titles in other libraries or consortia;
- availability of titles from commercial document delivery or other consortia;
- program needs and program changes on individual campuses;

- budgetary conditions at individual campuses and throughout the SUNY system.[3]

While the journal use study was in progress two of the campus grant managers participated in producing the ALA *Guide to Cooperative Collection Development*.[4] The *Guide* gives advice to prospective cooperators, including a list of "challenges" they must face, among which are the need for reallocation of resources, creation of new staffing patterns and new decision-making bodies. It points out the need for an infrastructure of rapid and cost-effective document delivery, acceptable on-site access and borrowing privileges, and adequate bibliographic control. It recommends shared collection development policy statements and joint collection assessment projects and counsels partners to adopt formal written agreements. To date the SUNY University Center partners have had only partial success in addressing these challenges.

The Centers have not implemented the Cooperative Journals Program. The four lists generated by the journal use study project have not been used collaboratively. There is little interest among the Center libraries in systematically reducing the number of subscriptions to low-use duplicated titles. Yearly consultation among the four campuses regarding new serials does not happen. Timing serials cancellation projects in concert to promote collaboration proved impossible. An up-to-date union list of serials is lacking, and a proposed database of serials decisions remains to be created. Instead, the chief collection development officers formed a council which is working on a monograph-based collection assessment project using AMIGOS software. At the behest of the library directors the council is also coordinating the purchase of (non-serial) expensive items from pooled funds. A proposal to appoint a policy advisory committee "to assist the library directors in planning an expanded program of cooperative collection development and resource sharing"[5] has not been acted upon.

The real success story of the CLR grant is probably SUNY Express, an interlibrary loan service that directs requests to the SUNY Center Libraries by preference and provides priority handling for Center clients. Costs are lower and turnaround time and fill rates have improved with the inauguration of this service, which now includes Syracuse and has been renamed Empire Express.

COST/BENEFIT STUDY

Following the journal use study, and consistent with the theme of using hard data to enlighten decision-making, the University Center libraries worked together successfully on another project designed to improve their knowledge of the economics of journal information delivery. Under the direction of Bruce R. Kingma, who holds a joint appointment from the SUNY Albany School of Information Science and Policy and the Department of Economics, a second study partially supported by the CLR focussed on high-cost/low-use journals in mathematics and the sciences. Kingma devised "A basic economic model to analyze the cost-efficiency of access to journal articles via three alternatives: journal subscriptions, consortium membership, and commercial document delivery."[6] "The model illustrates the importance of measuring not only the average cost of interlibrary loan by the participating libraries–i.e., the total cost divided by the number of transactions–but also the marginal cost, or cost per article requested through interlibrary loan. The study includes the opportunity cost to patrons, who, if access is provided by interlibrary loan, must wait for delivery. The results are examined in the context of the SUNY Express consortium, which provides priority interlibrary loan service to patrons. This model and estimates of interlibrary loan and journal subscription costs produce three decision rules based on the costs of the borrowing library, its patrons, and the costs to the lending library. The rules enable library directors to determine if journal subscription or interlibrary loan access is more economically efficient."[7] "The cost-efficiency of the decision to buy or borrow is based on the present value of future journal use, the marginal cost of consortium and commercial delivery, the fixed costs of delivery and subscriptions, and the value of time to patrons."[8] From these data the "tipping point," or number of uses at which access to a specific title by interlibrary loan is more cost-efficient than a subscription, may be calculated. Graphing the data on two axes makes the "tipping point" easy to see.[9]

Specific data from the Centers, when plugged into these equations, proved extremely interesting to the participants:

1. The average opportunity cost for a patron per article in the study was less than $2.
2. The average willingness to pay for priority delivery by patrons was about $2.50.
3. The economic cost of borrowing varied by method of delivery, and was calculated to be significantly less for SUNY Express than for other interlibrary loan or the least expensive commercial document delivery alternative studied.
4. The fixed cost of purchasing a subscription averaged about $63 per title and the marginal cost per use averaged less than $0.10.

It must be pointed out that the results presented in Kingma's study are specific to the four participating libraries at one point in time. Caution should be used in generalizing from them. "Other libraries should determine how closely their own costs of subscription and interlibrary loan–along with the level of patron use of the journals and opportunity cost of waiting for interlibrary loan access–are to the costs of the libraries in the study."[10]

The study concluded that for the Centers "Significant additional financial and economic savings can be achieved from increased use of interlibrary loan for access to scholarly journal articles" and "Consortium cost differences and current levels of journal subscription use suggest that at this time it is not worthwhile to consider joint collection development among the SUNY Express libraries."[11] Just as the decision about ownership or access to any title may change with new data inputs, these striking conclusions are subject to revision in light of new data. The value of a good model is that it can help decision-makers respond appropriately to changes in the environment.

The recommendation in favor of local collecting may also derive from pragmatic observation of what happened following the earlier journal use study. Despite this negativity, cooperation on journal resources among the Center partners is not a dead issue. The ALA Guide points out that cooperation calls on its practitioners to revise decision-making structures and to seek new methods of doing things. In 1995 SUNY Central convened the SUNY Contract Advisory Team, comprised of members from college and university libraries, to function on behalf of the entire SUNY system.

In July 1995 the State University of New York, the California State University, and the City University of New York joined in a venture called CETUS, the Consortium for Educational Technology for University Systems. This joint initiative in technology-assisted teaching, learning, and research announced that among its initial areas of concentration were "technology-based library resources and group purchasing/contracting opportunities." A task force comprised of librarians with broad consortial responsibilities was appointed by the new Consortium for Educational Technology for University Systems to do this.[12]

These two entities identify, review, and negotiate consortial licenses for electronic products to be accessed over the Internet. Products selected to date include OCLC FirstSearch and CARL Uncover Reveal. Proposals for other information services such as access to the full texts of journals offered by certain publishers are under consideration. The cost/benefit study did not include the option of electronic document delivery via the new WWW-based integrated information services that have appeared recently, nor did it include the electronic full text journal option. These would have added useful dimensions to the study, because it is with making decisions about them that the SUNY libraries are grappling today.

RETHINKING SUNY

While the cost/benefit decision rules per se have not been used in any University Center cancellation projects yet, and may never be, the study's conclusions may have influenced strategic thinking about cooperative collection development and document delivery. In the Fall of 1995 the New York State Legislature charged the SUNY Board of Trustees to report their plans by December 1, 1995 to "develop a multi-year comprehensive, system-wide plan to increase cost-efficiency." This has come to be known as "Rethinking SUNY."

A draft response written by an ad-hoc group of librarians and distributed by the SUNY Central Office of Library and Information Services offers insight into the thinking of some key SUNY librarians on the subject of document delivery and expensive and duplicated serials resources. The plan responds to a question left unanswered at the end of the Essen paper: What should be done with any financial "dividend" realized by the cancellation on principle of low-use and duplicated titles? Should it be used to staff interlibrary loan, to subsidize commercial document delivery, to subscribe to new unique paper journals, to purchase expensive microform sets, to acquire new electronic information resources?

The draft document listed seven concerns, of which two were pertinent to serials: "Electronic information resources are consuming a greater percentage of library acquisition budgets," and "Libraries need to employ more cost-efficient ways to receive copies of monographs and journal articles which are not available within the local collection." The solution proposed was that "SUNY establish a comprehensive document delivery strategy with a focus on delivering information directly to the end user whenever possible. . . . Local serials collections are likely to be replaced by less expensive document delivery."[13]

The document offered the following vision:

> As SUNY libraries reduce their reliance on locally owned books and journals, and as campuses offer more distance learning courses, innovative procedures for receiving and delivering traditional and electronic information must be accepted and deployed. Such procedures would include a standard interface to all SUNY library electronic catalogs, regionally mounted full text databases, and user-initiated interlibrary loan; cost effective ground transportation services, use of computer systems to send and receive electronic text and/or images of journal articles; contractual relationships with multiple commercial document suppliers and database vendors.[14]

The draft report was rejected by those for whom it was intended, the SUNY Council of Library Directors, less perhaps because of the content than because of how it was produced. Some of its provisions will see action eventually.

The *Final Report* of the first CRL project spoke of the University Centers Libraries' vision of institutional interdependence. "Each library would consider the users of the other three campuses as if they were its own users and endeavor to serve them as expeditiously as possible."[15] The four university libraries are now increasingly working in the broader context of the whole SUNY system and with CETUS, the largest academic consortium in the United States. We have already seen the fruits of this collaboration in the above discussion about negotiating consortial licenses.

CONCLUSION

The Essen paper described an "American model" for serials cooperation made up of the following steps:

1. Create a union list of serials
2. Assure the availability of reliable, user-initiated document delivery
3. Link catalogs and share other bibliographic databases electronically
4. Change the shape of the collections involved, assisted by journal use studies and collection assessment projects.[16]

Those like Maurice Line who subscribe to the idea that "it is questionable if cooperative acquisition schemes do, or can do, anything significant that cannot be, and is not, achieved without them,"[17] will not be disappointed to learn that the above plan was not fully implemented in the SUNY Centers. Despite the fact that the Centers' cost/benefit study demonstrated that serials cooperative collection development was "unjustified" at that point in time, significant cooperative collection development that might very well end up changing the shape of the participants' collections is taking place at the Center Libraries and within the entire SUNY system; it is now practiced on behalf of the entire SUNY system by those responsible for electronic information resources decisions.

NOTES

1. State University of New York. University Center Libraries. *Final Report to the Council on Library Resources on the Cooperative Planning Grant.* Albany, NY: The Libraries, 1993, pp. 5-6.

2. Suzanne Fedunok and Sharon Bonk, "Cooperative acquisition and new technologies for resource sharing: an American model." In: *Resource Sharing: New Technologies as a Must for Universal Availability of Information; Festschrift in honor of Hans-Peter Geh; Proceedings of the 16th International Essen Symposium, 1993.* (Publications of Essen University Library, 17). Essen: Universitaetsbibliothek Essen, 1994, pp. 35-50. See also Kate S. Herzog, "Final report of the CLR-funded journal use study." In: State University of New York. University Center Libraries. *Final Report to the Council on Library Resources on the Cooperative Planning Grant.* Albany, NY: The Libraries, 1993.

3. Suzanne Fedunok and Bonita Bryant, "SUNY University Centers cooperative journals program." In: State University of New York. University Center Libraries. *Final Report to the Council on Library Resources on the Cooperative Planning Grant.* Albany, NY : The Libraries, 1993.

4. Association for Library Collections and Technical Services. Collection Management and Development Section. Subcommittee on Guide to Cooperative Collection Development, *Guide to Cooperative Collection Development.* Chicago: American Library Association, 1994.

5. State University of New York. University Center Libraries, *Final Report,* p. 9.

6. B. R. Kingma, "Access to journal articles: A model of the cost efficiency of document delivery and library consortia." *Proceedings of the ASIS Annual Meeting* 31 (1994): pp. 8-16.

7. Bruce R. Kingma, *The Economics of Access versus Ownership: the Costs and Benefits of Access to Scholarly Articles via Interlibrary Loan and Journal Subscriptions. Final Report presented to the Council on Library Resources.* N.p., n.d, p. 4-5.

8. Ibid., p. 11.

9. Bruce Kingma with Suzanne Irving, "The economics of access versus ownership." *Journal of Interlibrary Loan, Document Delivery & Information Supply* 6(3) (1996).

10. Kingma, *The Economics of Access versus Ownership,* p. 5.

11. Ibid., p. ii-iii.

12. State University of New York, the California State University, and the City University of New York. Memorandum of Understanding dated July 22, 1995. Saratoga Springs, New York.

13. Carey Hatch, "Report presented to the SCLD and SUNYLA representatives Nov. 6, 1995." SUNYLA-L listserv November 13, 1995.

14. Ibid.

15. State University of New York. University Center Libraries, *Final Report,* p. iii.

16. Fedunok and Bonk, "Cooperative acquisition," p. 48.

17. Maurice B. Line, "National self-sufficiency in an electronic age." In: *Electronic Documents and Information: from Preservation to Access; Festschrift in Honor of Patricia Battin*; 18th International Essen Symposium 23 October-26 October 1995, Ahmed H. Helal, ed. (Publications of Essen University Library; 20) Essen: Universitaetsbibliothek, 1996, pp. 170-192.

Scientific Journal Usage
in a Large University Library:
A Local Citation Analysis

William Loughner

SUMMARY. Citation analysis is a helpful tool for evaluating academic library usage. When only the publications of local users are analyzed, the results are even more relevant to the local library. Manual collection of citations can be a time- and labor-intensive operation and has inhibited widespread use of local citation analysis. This study demonstrates how to use the *Science Citation Index* CD-ROM product and a personal computer to generate useful reports utilizing a much larger base of citations than previously has been possible. Moreover, the process is so relatively quick and easy that it can be run annually or whenever needed. In the study, over 35,000 citations from papers by scientific researchers at the University of Georgia were analyzed to generate reports useful for collection development. *[Article copies available for a fee from The Haworth Document Delivery Service: 1-800-342-9678. E-mail address: getinfo@haworth.com]*

INTRODUCTION

Local use studies in libraries are acknowledged as an important tool for evaluating library collections. In particular, studying the use

William Loughner is Physical Sciences Bibliographer, Science Library, University of Georgia, Athens, GA 30602 (E-mail: loughner@uga.cc.uga.edu).

[Haworth co-indexing entry note]: "Scientific Journal Usage in a Large University Library: A Local Citation Analysis." Loughner, William. Co-published simultaneously in *The Serials Librarian* (The Haworth Press, Inc.) Vol. 29, No. 3/4, 1996, pp. 79-88; and: *Serials Management in the Electronic Era: Papers in Honor of Peter Gellatly, Founding Editor of* The Serials Librarian (ed: Jim Cole, and James W. Williams) The Haworth Press, Inc., 1996, pp. 79-88. Single or multiple copies of this article are available for a fee from The Haworth Document Delivery Service [1-800-342-9678, 9:00 a.m. - 5:00 p.m. (EST). E-mail address: getinfo@haworth.com].

79

of periodicals is something that most libraries have attempted. However, the lack of agreement about the best way to take such a survey and how to interpret or use the results indicates that new methods might be beneficial.[1] This paper details a method developed at the University of Georgia employing the *Science Citation Index (SCI)*[2] to evaluate local scientific journal use. It does not measure journal use directly (that is, by observing, counting or asking) but uses citation analysis to give a powerful indicator of which scientific journals are being utilized by researchers at the University of Georgia.

Librarians and others have used citation analysis to evaluate scientific journals for much longer than *SCI* has been published, but the usefulness of general citation studies for a local library is still in dispute and may not accurately reflect actual use in that library. Kelland and Young review the long-standing unresolved discussion in the literature about "whether citations correlate with library use."[3] The published debate between Broadus and Line in 1985 is an exemplar of this discussion.[4-6] Broadus, considering the *Journal Citation Reports (JCR)*[7] produced by the Institute for Scientific Information (ISI), the publishers of *SCI,* and other citation studies, concludes that citation analysis correlates well with local library journal use: "If proper allowances are made, counts based on the *JCR* can be almost as good as expensive local studies for predicting use of periodicals in a given library."[8] Line contends that any such correlation is weakest among the lowest cited journals (where librarians need the most help) and one of his conclusions is that "citations reflect actual use imperfectly and so cannot be used with much confidence by librarians."[9] In an earlier paper, Line also writes that "no measure of journal use other than one derived from a local-use study is of any significant practical value to librarians."[10] During the past decade of budgetary and monetary fluctuations many librarians have taken Broadus' counsel and used general citation studies to help evaluate their collections, but have suffered from Line's doubts that only local studies are really useful.

One way to bridge these two viewpoints is to conduct a citation study that is also a local use study. If only the citations of local researchers undergo analysis, then the correlation of the result with actual local usage should be higher. A few studies have attempted the fusion of citation analysis and local use measurement using manual methods. McKimmie analyzed a sample of 2,995 citations over 3 years by faculty at New Mexico State University to help evaluate the collection.[11] Dykeman did a more extensive study of 13,982 citations from a one year output at the Georgia Institute of Technology to help study a declining collection.[12] Neal and Smith analyzed 1,837 citations from two years of work done at the branches of Pennsylvania State University.[13] McCain and Bobick conducted a multi-year study of a biology departmental library using 4,155 citations from journals and dissertations.[14] Because of the labor-intensive nature of manually collecting and collating large numbers of citations, these studies generally use small samples or involve small institutions. The more exhaustive Dykeman study mentioned "the considerable amount of staff time" that the project needed.[15]

METHODS

It is an interesting anomaly that the *SCI* has been used to produce many general citation studies, but it has not been applied to local library use studies. This study, however, uses *SCI* to analyze citations generated by scientific researchers only at the University of Georgia. Restricting the study to those publications indexed by *SCI* in 1994 produces a very large collection of 35,035 citations from 1,335 papers. Since most of the effort formerly performed manually is now expended by a personal computer, this study is easy to do in a short period of time. It can be replicated on an annual basis and can be easily used to compile multi-year reports.

The CD-ROM version of *SCI* is crucial to this study. I used the 1994 disk, although it is possible to use other years or combinations of years. The following procedure produces a list of the journals (and other publications) cited by University of Georgia scientific researchers during 1994. Each step is listed below and discussed in turn.

1. Locate all papers in *SCI* by local researchers.

SCI standardizes addresses and the CD-ROM version indexes the address field. *SCI* also lists multiple addresses so that the 1,335 papers include ones in which a local researcher is not necessarily the first author.

2. Download to a computer file all the citations from those papers.

This produces a large file so sufficient room on the hard drive of the computer is crucial before starting. The *SCI* CD-ROM search program takes a number of hours to locate and download the information. Fortunately computers are patient.

3. Edit each citation to remove all data except that pertaining to the publication.

A program written by the author in the BASIC programming language does the editing in this step. *SCI* standardizes the form of each citation so this is an easy task. For example, a citation might be:

PAULING-L-1949-SCIENCE-V110-P543

The BASIC program strips off all data through and including the date and also all data from the volume and page designations, if they exist, to the end of the citation. In the example above, this computer editing produces SCIENCE as the publication. Figure 1 shows some typical citations and the resulting publication.

4. Sort the list of publications into alphabetical order and combine identical items.

The same BASIC program sorts individual publications and combines identical items into a list that now also gives occurrences. This study has 35,035 citations which result in 7,084 unique publications.

5. Edit this list to combine all instances in which the same publication is referred to in different ways.

Step 4 would essentially end our task if not for the fact that a publication may be cited in various forms. The editors at ISI, the publisher of *SCI,* do an amazing job of reconciling most of these differences, especially for the often-cited publications, but it is inevitable that not all differences can be caught. An element of subjectivity enters here, because human judgment must decide that two different items on the list represent the same publication. However, many variations so obviously do represent the same publication (or at least the same title) that this combining is easy to do, though time-consuming. Figure 2 shows examples of groups of publication abbreviations that were combined into a single publication after step 4. Figure 3 shows part of the final list produced after this manual editing of this step.

6. Sort this list by occurrences to produce a second ranked list.

It is useful for the program to sort this alphabetical list of publications into a list ranked by publication occurrence. Figure 4 gives the beginning of this list, showing the most cited publications by our local researchers, and also a section from farther down the list.

RESULTS

The downloaded information from *SCI,* after computer manipulation, has produced two lists. The first is an alphabetical listing of all the publications, with occurrence numbers, cited by University of Georgia scientific researchers during 1994 (Figure 3). This list contains 7,084 publications, of which 4,364 were cited only once.

FIGURE 1. Extracting the publication from the citation.

APOSTOL-C-1986-APPROXIMATION-HILBER-V2
becomes: APPROXIMATION-HILBER

DAVIS-EL-1994-FUNDAM-APPL-NEMATOL-V17-P255
becomes: FUNDAM-APPL-NEMATOL

<ANON>-1980-EPA441180301-REP
becomes EPA441180301-REP

MIKHAILOV-BM-1965-IAN-SSSR-KH-P898
becomes: IAN-SSSR-KH

FIGURE 2. Groups of citation abbreviations that were combined into a single publication. This editing was done manually.

ACTA PAED-SCAN
ACTA-PAEDIATR-SCAND

AGR-HDB
AGR-HDB-USDA
USDA-AGR-HDB
USDA-HDB

LECI-NOTES-MATH
LECTURE-NOTES-MATH

MAR-ECOL-PROG-SER
MAR-ECOL-PROGR-SER
MARINE-ECOLOGY-PROGR

NEW-ZEAL-VET-J
NZ-VET-J

P-FLA-STATE-HORT-SOC
P-FLA-STATE-HORTIC-S

The second list is a ranking of the first by occurrence numbers (Figure 4).

One major purpose of usage studies, and the reason this study was done, is for collection evaluation. The implicit premise of presenting usage rates for local collections is that the higher the usage rate of a publication, the more that publication serves the users of the collection. The two lists give evidence of the relative usage of publications, most of them journals, by University of Georgia researchers. There can be little doubt, for example, that the *Journal of biological chemistry* is a very useful journal in our collection. (It received over 2% of all citations in 1994.) And surely a journal cited three times is much less useful to local researchers. Whenever the usefulness of a particular journal is queried, these lists, or more up-to-date versions of them, will provide relevant information.

This data can be further manipulated to provide other insights

FIGURE 3. Part of the alphabetical list of all publications cited by University of Georgia researchers in 1994. Over half the publications are cited only once.

HIST-RESOURCES-STUDY	1
HISTOCHEM-J	3
HISTOLOGY	3
HISTOLOGY-FOWL	2
HIV-AIDS-SURVEILLANC	1
HIVE-HONEY-BEE	1
HLTH-ED	1
HLTH-ED-Q	2
HLTH-ED-RES	2
HLTH-ENV-FACTORS-ASS	1
HLTH-FITNESS-PHYSICA	1
HLTH-IND-BEHAVIORAL	2
HLTH-PHYS	1
HLTH-PROMOTION-LABOR	1
HLTH-PROMOTION-PLANN	1
HLTH-PROMOTION-STUDI	1
HLTH-PSYCHOL	2

into the collection. For example, Figure 5 lists the approximate 1994 subscription costs of some of the University of Georgia's more expensive scientific journals (unnamed to protect the innocent) with their local citation counts. Even after considering the cautions and warnings of the next section of this paper, this is relevant data. Comparison of the 1994 lists with other years can provide information about changes in the relative importance of individual titles or particular subject areas. Certainly the list from 2004 should provide some interesting contrasts.

A common result of citation studies is the finding that a small number of publications account for most of the citations.[16] So it is no surprise that 2,720 publications (those cited more than once) receive 30,670 citations (87.5%). Our top 50 ranked publications (out of 7,084 total) receive 29% of all citations.

LIMITATIONS

Citation studies of any kind almost always produce interesting and suggestive results. Surely this explains their continuing appeal.

FIGURE 4. Parts of a ranked list of publications cited by University of Georgia researchers during 1994. Out of 7,084 publications so cited, 4,364 were cited only once.

1.	J-BIOL-CHEM	859
2.	J-AM-CHEM-SOC	692
3.	J-CHEM-PHYS	633
4.	P-NATL-ACAD-SCI-USA	477
5.	J-BACTERIOL	363
6.	NATURE	360
7.	SCIENCE	322
8.	BIOCHEMISTRY-USA	321
9.	APPL-ENVIRON-MICROB	311
10.	BIOCHIM-BIOPHYS-ACTA	231

. . .

69.	ACTA-CHEM-SCAND	76
	J-GEN-MICROBIOL	76
	THESIS-U-GEORGIA-ATH	76
72.	J-CHEM-SOC	75
73.	ARCH-BIOCHEM-BIOPHYS	74
	CARBOHYD-RES	74
75.	MED-SCI-SPORT-EXER	72
76.	J-NUTR	71
77.	MOL-CEL-BIOL	70
78.	EMBO-J	69
	GEOCHIM-COSMOCHIM-AC	69
80.	ANTIMICROB-AGENTS-CH	68

Yet for as long as researchers have studied citations, warnings and cautions have also appeared.[17] A general rehashing of these is not appropriate here. Sufficient to say all usage studies have their limitations and the major reasons that the study described in this paper should not be used in isolation are given below.

1. Only the citations of those local researchers who published during the given time period are counted. The uncited work that they also used and all the material used by those who did not publish (including undergraduates, for example) are not counted.
2. The time range over which items were cited is not considered. A journal may be cited primarily for work published in it 30

years ago or for work presented only recently. The rank of journals that have recently changed in importance will be improperly reflected. This problem might be corrected with more computer processing—retaining dates, for example—but the solution is rather more difficult and very recent usage (work being cited after *SCI* goes to press) is still missed.

3. Journals with a small number of papers will generally rank lower. This problem would include new journals and journals that have undergone name changes. Further research on individual publications can help overcome some but not all of this bias.

4. The importance of a journal will be inflated if it is cited frequently for only a small number of papers with most of its work ignored.

CONCLUSION

The results given here show that large-scale citation analysis is a practical way for the local library to measure journal usage. The *SCI* CD-ROM can be employed in an efficient and effective way to survey the citation patterns of local researchers and provide the

FIGURE 5. A few anonymous expensive journals with their approximate prices and local citation counts in 1994.

	Cost in 1994	Local citation count in 1994
Journal A	$9,000	39
Journal B	$9,000	14
Journal C	$6,500	179
Journal D	$5,000	3
Journal E	$5,000	192
Journal F	$4,500	41
Journal G	$4,000	27
Journal H	$4,000	9

librarian with the means to help evaluate the collection that those researchers use.

The author would be pleased to share the BASIC program used in this study with any requester.

REFERENCES

1. Barbara Lockett, ed., *Guide to the Evaluation of Library Collections*. (Chicago and London: American Library Association, 1989). 25 p.

2. *Science Citation Index with Abstracts*. (Philadelphia, PA: Institute for Scientific Information, 1992-). Compact disc ed.

3. John Laurence Kelland and Arthur P. Young, "Citation as a Form of Library Use," *Collection Management* 19, no. 1/2 (1994): 81-100.

4. Robert N. Broadus, "A Proposed Method for Eliminating Titles from Periodical Subscription Lists," *College and Research Libraries* 46, no. 1 (January, 1985): 30-35.

5. Maurice B. Line, "Use of Citation Data for Periodical Control in Libraries: A Response to Broadus," *Ibid.* 46, no. 1 (January, 1985): 36-37.

6. Robert N. Broadus, " On Citations, Use and Informed Guesswork: A Response to Line," *Ibid.* 46, no. 1 (January, 1985): 38-39.

7. *SSCI Journal Citation Reports* (Philadelphia, PA: Institute for Scientific Information, 1977-).

8. Broadus, "A Proposed Method," p. 33.

9. Line, "Use of Citation Data," p. 37.

10. Maurice B. Line, "Rank Lists Based on Citations and Library Uses as Indicators of Journal Usage in Individual Libraries," *Collection Management* 2, no. 4 (Winter, 1978): 313-316. (Quote on p. 313.)

11. T. McKimmie, *Communicating with Faculty about the Collection: Citation Analysis and Beyond* (Las Cruces, NM: New Mexico State University Library [1994]). 18 p. (ERIC document ED370536).

12. Amy Dykeman, "Faculty Citations: An Approach to Assessing the Impact of Diminishing Resources on Scientific Research," *Library Acquisitions: Practice & Theory* 18, no. 2 (Summer, 1994): 137-146.

13. James G. Neal and Barbara J. Smith, "Library Support of Faculty Research at the Branch Campuses of a Multi-Campus University," *Journal of Academic Librarianship* 9, no. 5 (November, 1983): 276-280.

14. Katharine W. McCain and James E. Bobick, "Patterns of Journal Use in a Departmental Library: A Citation Analysis," *Journal of the American Society for Information Science* 32, no. 4 (July, 1981): 257-267.

15. Dykeman, "Faculty Citations," p. 139.

16. Lockett, *Guide,* p. 13.

17. Tony Stankus and Barbara Rice, "Handle with Care: Use and Citation Data for Science Journal Management," *Collection Management* 4, no. 1/2 (Spring/Summer, 1982): 95-110.

Plugged-In Jell-O™:
Taught or Caught?

Esther Green Bierbaum

SUMMARY. In considering whether electronic serials should be "caught" informally or taught as a course or topics in various courses in the formal graduate professional program, the author compares the characteristics of print and electronic publications and the concomitant competencies reasonably required to deal with them; briefly examines the history of teaching serials; and then suggests modalities for instruction in electronic serials both for the future serialist and for the future librarian who will encounter them in the course of daily reader service. *[Article copies available for a fee from The Haworth Document Delivery Service: 1-800-342-9678. E-mail address: getinfo@ haworth.com]*

INTRODUCTORY MUSINGS

The bibliographic control of serial publications has been likened to "nailing Jell-O to the wall."[1] And that is just the print stuff.

What happens, then, when this virtually unmanageable universe of tangible, visible entities is rendered into an invisible and intangible virtual dimension? Is there a simile for dealing with those elusive and mutable ethereal blips we call e-journals?

Esther Green Bierbaum is affiliated with the School of Library and Information Science, The University of Iowa.

[Haworth co-indexing entry note]: "Plugged-In Jell-O™: Taught or Caught?" Bierbaum, Esther Green. Co-published simultaneously in *The Serials Librarian* (The Haworth Press, Inc.) Vol. 29, No. 3/4, 1996, pp. 89-103; and: *Serials Management in the Electronic Era: Papers in Honor of Peter Gellatly, Founding Editor of* The Serials Librarian (ed: Jim Cole, and James W. Williams) The Haworth Press, Inc., 1996, pp. 89-103. Single or multiple copies of this article are available for a fee from The Haworth Document Delivery Service [1-800-342-9678, 9:00 a.m. - 5:00 p.m. (EST). E-mail address: getinfo@haworth.com].

In point of fact, librarians have been regularly coping with blips for more than a decade. They call it bibliographic control; and the process is manifested daily in the databases of utilities and on the screens of local libraries.

How have they achieved that oxymoron? Ask experienced serialists and they recall that, early on, much was caught rather than taught. Essentially, electronic journals were there; serialists applied the principles they already knew. But catching cannot be forever; so academics among us have been looking at the business of teaching about the e-journal. Teach what? And how? And under what auspices and circumstances? My own journey through this thicket of questions begins with the assumption of an academic fief such as: "LIS 999. *Electronic Serial Publications.* 3 s.h. Graduate credit only. Lab fee." That it ends somewhere else may not be surprising— and the journey itself is rewarding. It begins with comparing the e-journal to its print cousin, not as to format alone, but also as to any necessary knowledge, skills or competencies that might be different from those required for the print universe. That exercise leads to a quick look at the history of teaching about serials and preparing serialists. With such a background we then can examine the possibilities for educational and training opportunities for professionals and professionals-to-be.

JOURNALS AND E-JOURNALS

Electronic journals sprouted in the wake of the computerization of libraries and offices. In the decade from the early 80s to the early 90s, they bloomed and flourished, so that by November of 1991, the CONSER database contained the records of over two hundred e-journals, most complete with ISSN.[2]

While the online version of electronic serials has lately been touched by Internet glamor, it is but one of several formats in which the digitized serial comes to the library. The first carrier of invisible content is the floppy disk, of both the 5 1/4 and 3 1/2 inch dimensions. An "issue" of the serial is usually self-contained on a floppy.

CD-ROM, the second medium, may also carry a single serial title (particularly if it is an annual). Additionally, it may be the alternative format for text that is also available in print. In this circumstance, the CD-ROM format is analogous to microfilm versions of printed texts.[3] Vendors are continually increasing the number and variety of printed serial titles available in full-text CD-ROM.

The third format is the online-accessible serial, often a by-product of the print publication process or a result of optical scanning. This electronic equivalent is available at an "address" or as an entity in a database. When the text–though, perhaps, not the look and feel–of the print version is electronically encoded, we have the multiple versions situation noted for some CD-ROMs.[4]

However, what is most likely to be called the e-journal (in a back-reference to e-mail) is the journal created for and normally accessible only through the online environment. It has a longer history than we might first conclude from the recent flurry of library and patron interest. Its remoter ancestry, of course, traces to the forums and discussion exchanges on Arpanet (begun in 1969) and its successor network, the Internet, as well as to the scientific community's report and preprint systems, already established in print and then vastly speeded up through electronic transmission.

The role of scientific immediacy can be seen in the debut of *The Online Journal of Current Clinical Trials*. Billed as the first formal scientific online journal, it was launched in October 1991 as a joint venture of OCLC (Online Computer Library Center) and AAAS (American Association for the Advancement of Science).[5] Refereed and peer-reviewed, and so validated as a recognized channel of intellectual exchange, this well-publicized example of the formal e-journal represented a radical departure for AAAS: an acknowledgement of new realities of "publication."

The earliest newsletters and "serials" (in the sense of continuing, even though intermittent, appearance) are lost to the mists of changing hardware and operating systems; many had already been proliferating in the decade before *Current Clinical Trials*. Many were–and still are–the etherized by-products of print publication; others, the individualistic creations of dedicated family room editors. Some grew up to be a *Hotwired*; others–with publishers who recognized a market when they saw one–focused on such fields as computers, technology, and investment. But it is the "'zines"–relatively easy (and cheap) to publish, novel and slightly zany, and with a wide appeal–which have in the last few years begun to twinkle like daisies along the Internet, even pulling in advertisers.[6] Not to be outdone, Microsoft is now proposing a serious-minded contender to the 'zine hegemony.[7]

And so now we have online magazines (not just journals, with the academic overtones implicit in that terminology), and—thanks to network connections—we can have them in all sorts of libraries. They have become a looming presence (or, perhaps, a flickering non-presence) for everyone.

JOURNALS AND E-JOURNALS:
KNOWLEDGE AND COMPETENCIES

When we compare electronic and print serials, one of the first matters to deal with is that very issue of non-presence, which has sometimes led to such conclusions as, "If they aren't in print, they aren't serials; so give 'em to the data people." AACR2, blessed with its Chapter 12, disposes of *that* notion; electronic serials do, indeed, exhibit the characteristics of seriality: issuance in parts at intervals; chronological or numerical designation; and the intention of continuing indefinitely. CONSER, for example, looks for a time-date stamp and enumeration as well as a title page screen.[8] Hence, whether the electronic serial joins the library's collection as blips from a network, or encoded on floppy disks or CD-ROMs, all the familiar protocols apply: acquisitions and payment, AACR2 and MARC, holdings and patron access.

That is, the familiar protocols apply, but with differences. Disk and disc versions, as physical carriers of content (however invisible it may be), are more closely related to print in terms of acquisitions—usually by order from a commercial source, with conventional payment procedures for the physical entity, a subscription for a specified period or number of entities, or a licensing arrangement. In contrast, the online serial is usually "acquired" through access via a network address, although some "subscriptions" (which are virtually licensing agreements) permit local downloading or the production of paper copy. On the other hand, many are still free (and fun) but debatable for library collections. While such organizations as the Association of College and Research Libraries (ARL) do a yeoman service in identifying electronic journals,[9] the e-serial universe, particularly the 'zine end of the spectrum, is strongly reminiscent of the alternative and underground press of two decades ago. A further concern in this daisy field is mutability of the publications as they pass from screen to screen: what–and where–is the original version?

Hence, the competencies of collection development and acquisitions apply equally to print and electronic serials; the decision to subscribe is a collection development issue. Even so, it may take extra sleuthing to locate and identify the electronic publications, plus a knowledge of computer systems, telecommunications, and different subscription procedures to acquire and pay for them.

Similarly, the competencies called for in cataloging both print and electronic serials are similar–but with differences. The conditions of seriality set forth in AACR2 are reflected in the ISBD and MARC formats, which are straightforward enough. Such variances as the GMD [computer file], the statement of electronic format in the "collation" (300 field), and the notation of online address or other access mode are just that–variances. Local peculiarities, however, such as the existence of downloaded print copies and the hosting arrangements for CD-ROMs, require careful notes and holdings data. A final resolution of the multiple versions question should allow the integrated MARC format to be applied in such a way as to enable the patron to identify both print and electronic versions from one bibliographic record, while the holdings statements should make clear which is which–and where.

Thus bibliographic description and local access data will require skills in applying MARC and integrated MARC formats, and in developing holdings statements. Copy cataloging will require the ability to supply local data and to make judgments regarding format representation, linking fields, and such amplifications as contents notes. To a large extent, however, these "extra" skills are agency-specific; cataloging principles are unchanged.

The patron seeking to identify and access an electronic journal may enjoy–or be confounded by–the fruits of bibliographic control, and turn to reader services for assistance. And just as it is necessary in the print world to help the patron identify the serial volume, number and date, so in the electronic world, these data, plus the mechanics of hardware and online addresses are part of the reference encounter. The cataloger's competencies extend to the reference encounter through on-screen guides, the fullness and accuracy of the description, and location and access information. In some libraries more than others, the work and decisions of technical services and serials librarians are discussed with the reference staff, who must know enough about serials to interpret to and create connections for the reader. Which is to say, seriality is not just for serialists–a thought we shall return to later.

The electronic condition of publication does, indeed, introduce Jell-O-nailing challenges–but hardly to the extent of warranting the LIS 999 solution posited early on. It seems to me that the question of how–or even whether–the management of electronic serials can be taught is an extension of the older debate over whether and how serials in general can be taught. A brief look at this debate should help in formulating an answer.

EDUCATION: THE GRADUATE PROGRAM

There are three principal venues for library information science (LIS) education: the professional program of the graduate school in LIS; on-the-job training in a particular library for a particular professional position; and continuing education designed to enhance and update skills and competencies and to prepare the librarian for professional advancement. In general, the first setting aims at preparing LIS professionals; the other two, at creating and sustaining serialists.

In the professional school setting, serials can be taught in three modes: as a separate course; as a major element in another course (such as technical services); or as a topic in various courses (such as collection development and reference). Historically, "serials" has not fared well as a solo act. In 1974, when Benita Weber surveyed serials librarians,[10] 13% of the 62 accredited graduate schools offered a course "in serials"; and 3 of these 8 folded serials into a course in technical services. Six years later, in 1980, the situation had improved, as reported by Hanson and Linkins.[11] Of their 45 respondents, 40% reported an elective course in serials, while 82% had encountered serials as a topic included in one or more courses. A few years later, in 1984, Stine[12] found that a similar proportion

(39% of 43 responding library schools) offered a course in serials. Stine, however, was not enthused at the level of "adequacy" of serials preparation; she suggested lodging serials topics in *required* courses so that "library schools can insure that their graduates will be prepared for positions as serials librarians."[13]

In 1986, Soper[14] gathered data on a narrower aspect of serials management, that of cataloging. Of her 53 respondent schools, 30% offered separate serials courses; 49% perceived serials as sufficiently different as to require special treatment in the curriculum; and 47% felt that automation–far from solving everything–"increased the need for more preparation [for serials]."[15] Soper herself rather disputed this latter conclusion, noting that "graduates should be equally familiar with both [serials and monographs]."[16]

Essentially then, the choice in formal education for serials librarianship has been and still is between offering a separate course in serials, or including serials-related topics in various courses. Hewitt reports that the separate course was the mode preferred by 86% of LIS students at the University of North Carolina at Chapel Hill, a choice based on the students' sensitivity to matters of "appropriate academic content"–that is, *amount* of content and potential breadth and depth of treatment.[17] Academic content was also a concern of the UK Serials Group Conference, meeting at the University of Durham, March 21-24, 1983,[18] and of the Phinazee Symposium in 1992.[19] It was also the focus of proposed models and syllabi for courses offered in Australia.[20,21]

In order to discern present trends, I examined recent or current catalogs from 47 accredited schools, finding that a separate course in serials is offered by 58% of these schools, an increase over previous reports. In half of the remaining 42%, serials-related topics are listed within other courses–principally technical services, and advanced cataloging. In one instance a course in electronic technologies takes note of online serials. However, heed has not been paid to Stine; core courses are not the vehicles for serials-related topics.

Given the 12-course design of most LIS curricula, and the increasing amount of knowledge deemed necessary for the infamous Day One, it is unlikely that the specific-serials-course *vs.* serials-topics-in-other-courses will be resolved entirely in favor of the single course, even though it enjoys a slight edge in this sample.

Boydston, for example, felt her technical services and advanced cataloging courses served her well.[22] Yet, as Hewitt's students noted, the need for "an in-depth knowledge of serials . . . [is] pervasive in research and special libraries."[23]

Largely neglected in the debate on the professional preparation of serialists–save for Soper's equal familiarity clause–is the question of instilling a general knowledge of seriality. As already noted in the discussion of e-serial competencies, reader services librarians continue to play an important–and perhaps even more active–role in connecting the reader with the serial. It is reference librarians who must daily deal with the decisions and bibliographic records generated by serialists and catalogers, and whose responsibilities and necessary range of competencies have increased in the electronic environment.

Hence, it seems to me that it is reasonable to expect that the professional program should furnish sufficient knowledge about the role and management of serials in libraries so that *all* librarians can deal with them on a daily basis. In fact, Koenig's proposed "four components . . . of a serials concentration in library education" are equally valid for other LIS specializations:

- knowledge of the capabilities of computers and telecommunications systems . . . ;
- knowledge of scholarly communications . . . ;
- complementary quantitative skills for decision making; and
- knowledge of basic economic principles.[24]

Additionally–and ideally–there should also be provision for more detailed and extensive coursework in serials librarianship for those planning to pursue that area or to enter special and scientific librarianship.

EDUCATION: ON-THE-JOB TRAINING

On-the-job training, the second delivery mode and the orientation Carter terms "learning routines and procedures specific to the job,"[25] is not dealt with as extensively in the literature. But we should not conclude that it is unimportant. For example, Osmus provides details of such training from the manager's viewpoint; Boydston, from the trainee's.[26] It is evident that the experience was mutually beneficial. A more structured training mode was reported from the 1990 NASIG (North American Serials Interest Group) by Meiseles.[27] Here the emphasis was on departmental and training objectives.

Beyond the formal offerings of local training, Carter[28] notes that constant reading is also part of on-the-job and continuing education, while Soper[29] urges the serials novitiate to join library association serials committees, sub-committees, and organizations such as NASIG.

EDUCATION: PROFESSIONAL DEVELOPMENT

Such organizational memberships can also be considered part of the third aspect of professional education, that of continuing education, or professional development. While the serials librarian is often largely on his or her own in this enterprise, such authors as Leonhardt[30] and Rast[31] offer guidance in seeking and finding such opportunities. Continuing education opportunities have greatly expanded in the past decade, as a glance at the programs for ALA and NASIG conferences and those for regional and state meetings will confirm.

Another aspect of professional development is library-related research. Boydston reports that 57% of the serials catalogers responding to her survey are encouraged in research efforts by their administrators, particularly with released time.[32] The whole area of e-journals lies ready for research; questions of cost effectiveness, promotion, reader preferences in access and delivery format–all these require exploration with the same diligence that the question of the curricular status of serials education was explored ten and fifteen years ago. Van Goethem[33] has nominated the electronic journal as "the third crisis for serialists." Ironically, e-journals are often touted as the alleviation of–if not the solution to–Van Geothem's first and second crises: escalating journal costs;[34] and crumbling paper.[35] But until more research is conducted and more experience is acquired, we cannot be sure.

Nor should continuing education be devoted solely to matters serial. Hunter[36] suggests that cost accounting, marketing, and strategic planning models are worthwhile courses, and that serials librarians should develop skills in negotiation, product development, research and analysis, and management information systems. Whatever its form, as Carter observed, "Continuing education should be seen as a way of life."[37]

ELECTRONIC JOURNALS: CAUGHT OR TAUGHT?

It is conceivable that we could undertake another debate about including electronic serials in the same course settings as serials in general or in their own, separate "LIS 999" course–conceivable, but unrealistic; e-journals are another format, but serials nonetheless. At the other end of the education spectrum we could argue that e-serials will be caught on the job; let the local library do its local thing. But the local catching still requires a net, some wider basis of understanding within which to fold the local instruction.

Hence, at the end of my e-Jell-O journey through formats and history, I must argue that electronic serials should indeed be taught, and taught in each of the three modes: formal graduate programs, in-house training, and profession development. Because the latter two settings are individualized and also dependent upon the first, I shall deal primarily with my conclusions about the means of teaching about electronic serials in the graduate program.

In the classroom setting, if seriality is accorded its own course or a portion of a technical services course, the electronic format ought to take its place with the print. Future serialists will then be well-served with a broader and deeper treatment, and should be ready to develop in-house training programs for serials and reference staff, and guides and aids for readers. They should also be prepared to undertake their own continuing professional development.

But my journey has convinced me of something else: that serials–whether print or electronic–are too important to be left to serialists. The complexity of the daisy field, the issues arising in allocating resources from print to electronic formats, and the level and type of reader services required, indicate that all future librarians, no matter what information setting or specialization they are contemplating, should be well acquainted with e-Jell-O, if not necessarily the art of nailing it. Hence, even when seriality enjoys its separate and specific course, there are numerous points at which electronic serials should be introduced; this is certainly the situation when seriality is scattered topically among other courses.

The "core" courses are neglected but ideal vehicles for these topics. In cataloging, the e-serial is a vivid example of applying the criteria of seriality to a non-print format. The functionality of integrated MARC in the instance of non-print serials becomes apparent: integration allows the cataloger to follow the AACR2 protocol of describing the serial aspect in Chapter 12 and the format in the appropriate medium-specific chapter.[38]

Issues and decisions for collection development include selecting the electronic titles, timing of their introduction to the collection, determining the suitable electronic format, and then deciding whether to maintain print and electronic versions. Matters of editorship and sponsorship, quality, and validity (including refereed status) are also aspects of collection development. Additionally, the concept of validity concerns online text modification and whether the library's "copy" is the base copy–or if there indeed is a base copy of the original, unmodified text.

Bibliographic control and user access–topics within the purview of courses in cataloging, technical services, and reader services–are vital to e-serials. Delivery mode, whether through online access via a network or central data service, or as datadisks, must be interpreted from the notes and holdings areas, and dictates in turn the degree and level of staff help that may be necessary, and the hardware the library must provide. User education, the transfer of paper-based skills to the electronic world, and the degree of reader self-sufficiency we should expect to develop, all are lively issues in reference and bibliography courses.

Management courses can tackle such matters as developing user acceptance, figuring the cost base (staff training time, staff time in user instruction, new computers, extra communication lines), and reallocating resources, particularly staff.[39] Topics such as the evaluation and selection of computers and other hardware, telecommunication access, Internet and other network connections, and the choice of controlling software and linkage to CD-ROM storage are all within the purview of information science or information technology courses.

Elective courses other than serials and technical services are also points of contact with electronic journals. Type-of-library courses, courses in publishing and publishing history, telecommunications, age-specific materials and service courses, and facilities design all present opportunities to introduce electronic serials to professionals-in-training. In addition to introducing e-serials as aspects and topics within courses, LIS graduate programs also can offer such instruction as part of internships and practica, and in workshops and continuing education programming.

All these things *can* happen; whether they will happen depends upon the alertness of the faculty to new developments in the field, their willingness to incorporate more elements into a crowded curriculum and crammed courses, the technology and electronic and online resources available, and–at least initially–the presence of an electronic advocate.

Something else important can take place in the nurturing environment of the graduate program, where real-world meters are not running: here electronic serials can also be *caught,* and caught by experimentation and exploration–that is, by creative messing around. Whether the approach is through a lab exercise, a paper or project assignment, or whetted curiosity, students should have the opportunity and be encouraged to surf, to cruise, to poke around. For there are things in the online world we wot not of, and which can only be experienced, not read about, and not memorized.[40]

E-JELL-O AND FUTURE WAVES

Libraries are in the midst of a seachange. We all want to believe that the outcome will be wonderful, however strange the process may seem just now. Whether or not the "national electronic library"[41] comes to pass, there are certain realities librarians will face. One is the changing nature of publishing, as exemplified by the OCLC-AAAS partnership in the scientific arena, and the entry of Microsoft into the current commentary field. As Hawkins points out, the library has a role in legitimizing and encouraging the electronic journal.[42] While the scholarly journal is the particular concern of academic and many special libraries, public libraries can, through careful selection and promotion of online magazines, encourage relevance, liveliness, and variety amidst the 'zines, at the same time serving the interests of their readers.

Another reality is the changing nature of periodicals in the electronic environment, with the real possibility of their deconstruction into their component articles.[43] Will serials then become dichotomized into print and online, with different audiences for each? Will the library "legitimize" itself out of the print realm?

Stones cast into a pond cause waves everywhere; the introduction of electronic serials affects all the rest of the library's functions and services. The challenge in teaching future serialists and their colleagues is to help them perceive electronic serials (and other things we have not thought of yet) neither as threats to the orderliness of the bibliographic world, nor as lifelines to institutional survival. Rather, each stone must be an integral element in the library's continuing mission to collect, preserve, and make accessible the records of humankind. The ethereal blips of *Hotwire* have the same purpose as the bound volumes of *National Geographic*: to inform, to entertain, to inspire.

And so in my journey after e-Jell-O, I rediscovered the truth that librarianship is all of piece; that when we teach some particular aspect (such as electronic serials), it must be taught as part of the whole. Ranganathan had it right:

"The library is a growing organism."[44]

NOTES AND REFERENCES

1. This oft-quoted analogy is itself difficult to nail. The author would appreciate information about the first citation. Interestingly, a cultural or linguisitic mistranslation had Woodworth executing an even more daunting feat, that of nailing "jelly." *See:* David P. Woodworth, "Serials Education; or, How to Nail Jelly to the Wall," in *The Future of Serials: Publication, Automation and Management* [10th conference proceedings] (Essen, Germany: International Association of Technological University Libraries, 1983), pp. 201-211.

2. Julia C. Blixrud, "CONSER and Electronic Serials," *CONSER,* Number 22 (January 1992):9-11.

3. Archivists, however, do not yet regard CD-ROM as a stable medium.

4. And, as Tenopir notes, libraries may be paying twice. See: Carol Tenopir, "Electronic Access to Periodicals," *Library Journal* 118/4 (1 March 1993):54-55.

5. Cynthia Lollar, "AAAS Launches Electronic Journal and New Publication Push," *Science* 253 (27 September 1991):1561.

6. The 'zines are fascinating and numerous enough to attract the attention of such observers of the contemporary scene as *Time*; see: *Time* 146/10 (4 September 1995):64.

7. Bart Ziegler, "On-Line Magazines Get Some Respect from Kinsley-Microsoft Webzine Plan," *The Wall Street Journal* (Midwest edition) 77/21 (Monday, 13 November, 1995):B1.

8. Blixrud, "CONSER and Electronic Serials," p. 3.

9. Lisabeth A. King, *Directory of Electronic Journals, Newsletters and Academic Discussion Lists,* 4th ed. (Washington, DC: Association of Research Libraries, 1994).

10. Benita M. Weber, "Education of Serials Librarians: A Survey," *Drexel Library Quarterly* 11/3 (July 1975):72-81.

11. Elizabeth Hanson and Germaine Linkins, "Serials Education in Library Schools," *Journal of Education for Librarianship* 23/2 (Fall 1982):83-95.

12. Diane Stine, "The Adequacy of Library School Education for Serials Librarianship," *Illinois Libraries* 67/5 (May 1985):448-452.

13. Stine, "The Adequacy," p. 449.

14. Mary Ellen Soper, "The Education of Serials Catalogers," *The Serials Librarian* 12/1-2 (1987):169-179.

15. Soper, "The Education," p. 175.

16. Soper, "The Education," p. 177.

17. Joe A. Hewitt, "Education for Acquisitions and Serials Librarianship: The Students' View," *Library Acquisitions: Practice and Theory* 11/3 (1987): 185-194.

18. D. P. Woodworth, "Serials Education," *The Serials Librarian* 73/3 (Spring 1983):63-65.

19. Ruth C. Carter, "Education for Serials: A Presentation at the Phinazee Symposium," *Cataloging and Classification Quarterly* 16/3 (1993):59-69.

20. G. E. Gorman, "The Education of Serials Librarians in Australia: A Proposed Course in Serials Librarianship," *The Serials Librarian* 17/1-2 (1989):45-67.

21. The question of amount and depth of course content is a real one in the university setting, where a certain degree of rigor and intellectual content is expected. Where the 3-hour course pattern is rigidly observed, neither "Acquisitions" nor "Serials" can be justified under graduate course criteria; where one-hour courses and modules are permitted, the stand-alone course is more feasible. The author has included serials as a four-week unit within a 15-week technical services course, and also as a one-day, 5-hour workshop. The latter presentation, highly focused for practitioners, concentrated on MARC and MARC integration, electronic serials, and "futuring."

22. Lori L. Osmus and Jeanne M. K. Boydston, "A Tale of Two Serials Catalogers: Their Education and Training," *Cataloging and Classification Quarterly* 7/4 (Summer 1987):95-108.

23. Hewitt, "Education for Acquisitions," p. 191.

24. Michael E. D. Koenig, "Education for Serials Librarianship: What Are the Not So Obvious Basic Components?" *Education for Information* 3/3 (September 1985):237-246.

25. Carter, "Education for Serials," p. 67.

26. Osmus and Boydston, "A Tale. . . . "

27. Linda Meiseles, "The Do's and Don't's of Serials Training," *The Serials Librarian* 19/3-4 (1991):217-219.

28. Carter, "Education for Serials," p. 67.

29. Soper, "The Education," p. 176.

30. Thomas W. Leonhardt, "Introducing Serials Education," *The Serials Librarian* 10/1-2 (Fall 1985-Winter 1986):211-214.

31. Elaine K. Rast, "Formal Continuing Education for Serials," *Illinois Libraries* 67/5 (May 1985):453-458.

32. Jeanne M. K. Boydston, "Continuing Education and Staff Development Among Serials Catalogers," *The Serials Librarian* 22/1-2 (1992):17-38.

33. Jeri Van Goethem, "Education for Serials: A Practitioner's View," *Cataloging & Classification Quarterly* 16/3 (1993):71-77.

34. Paul Metz, "Serials Pricing and the Role of the Electronic Journal," *College and Research Libraries* 52/4 (July 1991):315-327.

35. Marion L. Buzzard and John H. Whaley, "Serials and Collection Development," *Drexel Library Quarterly* 21/1 (Winter 1985):37-49.

36. Karen A. Hunter, "The Future of Serials Librarianship," *Serials Review* 16/2 (Summer 1990):60-61.

37. Carter, "Education for Serials," p. 67.

38. The technical aspects of downloading electronic texts to the institutional mainframe and creating local MARC records have been treated in the literature. See, for example, Gail McMillan, "Technical Processing of Electronic Journals," *Library Resources & Technical Services* 36/4 (October 1992):470-477; and Edward Gaynor, "Cataloging Electronic Texts: The University of Virginia Library Experience," *Library Resources & Technical Services* 38/4 (October 1994):403-413. On the other hand, there are arguments for letting the journals simply exist "as files in the Internet," saving physical and local storage space: Patricia Sayre McCoy, "Technical Services and the Internet," *Wilson Library Bulletin* 69/7 (March 1995):37-40.

39. Even without a subscription fee, costs are incurred! See: Gail McMillan, "Technical Processing," p. 477.

40. McCoy, "Technical Services," p. 40.

41. Brian L. Hawkins, "Planning for the National Electronic Library," *EDUCOM Review* 29/3 (May-June 1994):19-29.

42. Hawkins, "Planning," p. 27.

43. Walt Crawford & Michael Gorman, *Future Libraries: Dreams, Madness, & Reality* (Chicago: American Library Association, 1995), p. 68.

44. S. L. Ranganathan, *The Five Laws of Library Science,* 2nd ed. reprinted (Bangalore: Sarada Ranganathan Endowment for Library Science, 1988).

CONSER:
A Member's Perspective
of an Evolving Program

Martha Hruska

SUMMARY. This article describes the perspective of a CONSER member (University of Florida Libraries) weighing the benefits of continued participation in this cooperative cataloging program during a time of operational reassessment and change. The author maintains that CONSER's cooperative history can work to enable its members to integrate the agenda of the program with local priority issues, in the process, improving the quality of treatment of those issues. Electronic serials cataloging is cited as the kind of issue that benefits from discussion and cooperative projects among expert colleagues. *[Article copies available for a fee from The Haworth Document Delivery Service: 1-800-342-9678. E-mail address: getinfo@haworth.com]*

Since its beginning in the 1970s, the CONSER program has built an authoritative and fairly comprehensive database of bibliographic records for serial publications. The database is, and has been, the product and focal point of the genuinely cooperative efforts of the program members. Indeed, the CONSER acronym (and program goal) evolved from the Conversion of Serials Project to the Coop-

---

Martha Hruska is Associate Director for Technical Services at the George A. Smathers Libraries of the University of Florida, Gainesville, FL 32611.

[Haworth co-indexing entry note]: "CONSER: A Member's Perspective of an Evolving Program." Hruska, Martha. Co-published simultaneously in *The Serials Librarian* (The Haworth Press, Inc.) Vol. 29, No. 3/4, 1996, pp. 105-112; and: *Serials Management in the Electronic Era: Papers in Honor of Peter Gellatly, Founding Editor of* The Serials Librarian (ed: Jim Cole, and James W. Williams) The Haworth Press, Inc., 1996, pp. 105-112. Single or multiple copies of this article are available for a fee from The Haworth Document Delivery Service [1-800-342-9678, 9:00 a.m. - 5:00 p.m. (EST). E-mail address: getinfo@haworth.com].

erative Online Serials Program. In this paper, I will discuss how this cooperative nature of the operations and the governance of CONSER work to integrate the program with the local serials cataloging at the University of Florida Libraries.

From the perspective of one of the full level members, CONSER participation still works for us because it complements our own serials cataloging. The University of Florida Libraries continue to participate as a CONSER member because we can do so actively, with tangible and productive results, and because we have blended the requirements of the program with our business of ongoing serials cataloging.

Presently, the kind of traditional serials cataloging upon which the CONSER program is based is threatened on a number of counts. The converged threats posed by libraries' declining power to maintain serials subscription levels, the subsequent decrease in 'copy' serials cataloging, the decline in serials cataloging staffs, and the burgeoning of digital publications, which are both serial and dynamic in nature, demand we adapt both the content and the methods of the program. For CONSER to continue to set a coordinated standard for organized access and bibliographic control of serial publications, the focus of the program needs to shift. Fortunately, the program is a cooperative and is structured to accommodate incremental change. While it remains to be seen if the program can adapt as quickly as the Internet age may require, the questions CONSER members choose to consider, and the solutions proposed, are the responsibility of each of us who are members of the program. At such a changeable time, CONSER provides a seasoned forum of expertise for collaborative problem solving and concrete action.

In preparing this article, I reviewed the 1991 *Serials Review* Balance Point column entitled "CONSER: Cons and Pros, or, What's in it for Me?"[1] This column explored the benefits and the obstacles to CONSER participation, as seen by members, libraries who have decided against membership, and OCLC.

It seems that the issues have not changed, but a fair amount of progress has been made on them, because the program is structured to work as an open system and manages to accomplish what its participants want it to. Over the last few years,

- cataloging simplification efforts have cut down on the Library of Congress Rule Interpretations applying to serials;
- a core bibliographic record for serials has been identified;
- a CONSER-Enhance type membership category has been approved;
- for OCLC participants, at least, CONSER contributions no longer require separate procedures.

The somewhat intangible, but nevertheless extraordinary, bonus of working with a human network of trusted colleagues on a common objective continues as strongly as ever.

At a time of continually scrutinizing cataloging operations, we consider CONSER membership worthwhile because: (1) our ongoing serials cataloging can routinely be contributed to the database; and (2) we can influence and contribute to shaping program goals and initiatives as needs in our institution and environment incrementally change.

Our current serials cataloging can routinely be contributed to the CONSER database.

For the foreseeable future, the University of Florida Libraries expect to continue to acquire printed serial publications, particularly from Third World countries, which are not routinely cataloged by other Anglo-American libraries. Because much of this literature is integral to academic program commitments of the University, the Libraries will make it a priority to hire staff with the expertise to select, mediate, and provide access to these language and subject areas.

Given our initial CONSER and NACO training and the interactive nature of CONSER Operations, it has become routine that the original serials cataloging we have to do is contributed as a new CONSER record. While the University of Florida is not significantly increasing its subscriptions to new serials or periodicals, more publications from arrearages (as well as 'grey' literature) can be cataloged as we utilize the kinds of streamlining options enabled by CONSER's cataloging simplification initiatives. Greater depth and cataloging coverage of the more fugitive materials will benefit the greater library community. Renewed efforts to build cooperative collections and to share scarce resources effectively depend on shared databases with good bibliographic control and comprehensive coverage. Only in this way, will the greater library community be able to share access to the difficult materials we cannot, and should not, all collect.

Through a process of continual refinements to our own local workflows and, especially, as NACO and CONSER submissions have both been accommodated via OCLC inputting, the process of creating CONSER catalog records has become simply the way we do what we need to catalog, and is no more cumbersome than what would be required merely to create a new local catalog record.

The trend toward further cataloging simplification is, nevertheless, critical to our long-term staffing commitments. Our aim is to shift the staff resources which have been required to process core collection materials and to reduce those which have been required to create descriptive cataloging records to positions which better integrate selection, organization and referral services, especially for ephemeral and electronic literature. Although both LCRI review and the option of cataloging core records "introduce a more flexible approach to record requirements, relying on cataloger's judgment and local interpretation in a number of areas,"[2] the complexity still involved in establishing a name authority (NACO) record does not yet easily lend itself to a part-time assignment for an area/subject specialist.

The quality of the CONSER database enables us to utilize existing records with a minimum of review, by entry level paraprofessional staff trained to detect title changes and other problems requiring higher level staff review. Insofar as there is still a fair amount of duplication in core serial collections, we share the fairly common experience of encountering CONSER records that need to be upgraded: to add LC Classification number, subject heading(s), or to denote a change in the publication pattern. So we fully support the new, fifth, membership category, proposed and approved at the November 1995 CONSER Policy meeting. This new category will be a CONSER Enhance-type which will enable qualified members at this level to upgrade authenticated CONSER records. This will further distribute the responsibility for ongoing maintenance of the database. In theory, at least, this should keep the database more authoritative in a more timely way, and further free other members to focus on more new contributions.

We can influence and contribute to shaping program goals and initiatives as needs in our institution and environment incrementally change.

The CONSER membership constitutes a very successful and long running cooperative cataloging venture. This seems especially significant, because for all of its institutional members, the bibliographic control of serial publications has always been but one component of a multi-faceted library operation. Like any other good group effort, the product created has been much greater than the sum of its parts. The database which has resulted and the standards which have been established and well documented for serials cataloging have benefited the larger library community. As noted just after its first decade of operation, "libraries using the CONSER data base usually experienced substantial savings in cataloging personnel time and [obtained] access to extensive bibliographic information for their serials."[3] Over the next decade, the database continued to grow as a result of ongoing retrospective conversion projects among the members. CONSER was founded as a results-oriented project and has continually maintained that sense of product throughout its history.

Through common training programs, frequent interactive communications on both operational and policy questions, and regular meetings of the members, the program has been able to maintain its focus on issues relating to the bibliographic control of serials. Until recently many of these issues have been relatively easy to isolate in our institutions. Our staffs, budgets, and operations normally have been organized to deal with serials and periodicals separately from books and other resources. Now, however, it is becoming more difficult for many of us member libraries to maintain this kind of distinction along traditional lines for a number of reasons. For one, our materials budgets are generally stagnant or worse in the face of escalating prices for science/technology/business journals, and pressures to purchase more resources in (frequently costlier) electronic or digitized formats. Another reason is that many of these electronic/digitized resources, in fact, blur the serial/monograph distinction. Many electronic publications are continually updated or issued, electronic looseleafs, so to speak. With the advent of MARC format integration, serials will no longer be treated as a separate format. Seriality will simply be treated as a type of publication pattern, a characteristic of any medium or format. This means there will no longer be a separate MARC format for serials. Decisions regarding appropriate cataloging treatment will depend more on an institution's commitment to collect and archive a title than on the publication pattern of a title. Virtually all libraries will need to rethink staffing assignments and many of us who are CONSER members are finding we can no longer afford the luxury of professional staff exclusively assigned to cataloging serials and periodicals. Finally, many of us trying to administer technical services operations in our libraries need to coordinate our national cataloging program commitments. We cannot necessarily afford to administer separate sets of staff resources to participate in CONSER and the Program for Cooperative Cataloging (PCC) with its BIBCO, NACO, Series and Subject Cataloging components. In order to make, and then maintain, commitments to these, it is important that the training time and obligations for these programs remain reasonably well integrated, as in the case of NACO and CONSER.

As noted earlier, libraries will continue to acquire and collect serial literature for the foreseeable future even though the numbers of traditional print subscriptions may decrease. At any rate, the need to provide bibliographic access to these resources will not go away. However, the competing demands for limited library resources will increase. It is at this juncture that each of us who are full CONSER members need to assess the institutional costs and benefits of continuing in the program. In doing so, we can either assume the program itself will remain unchanged while our situations evolve, or we can assume the program will likewise evolve as our institutional priorities do. Either scenario is equally possible. After all, this is a membership organization and the program agenda is determined by what all the members have the interest and energy to do. Active participation in the program seems to work best for those of us member libraries when, as with current cataloging, these program activities coincide with our institutional priorities. The current CONSER agenda reflects the membership's desire to be more inclusive, more responsive and more project-oriented. The result should make responsibility for the bibliographic database broader and more distributed among the cataloging community. The current 'hot' issue on the agenda is electronic serials; a CONSER task force is assembling an action plan for the program to provide leadership on an issue challenging each of our libraries.

Digital resources, especially serials, do not fit well into any of our library acquisitions, check-in, and cataloging routines. Libraries are all grappling with the changes these entail. The opportunity to participate in CONSER's deliberations on this common challenge is an additional benefit of membership. As a participant, one is in a position to benefit from viewpoints and the varied experiences of colleagues. One also has the opportunity to influence direction on policy decisions in such a way that these may adapt as needed to a changing environment and that the policies of the program continue to mesh with local practices.

Since the November 1986 CONSER Management Retreat, the program has set a goal to "support and promulgate standards and establish necessary standardized practices for the bibliographic control of serials."[4] As Linda Bartley explained in another article, the goals set at this time marked CONSER's Phase 4, an era of synthesis, defining the program more broadly than simply in terms of the database product. The objective to play a role in setting standards for serials acknowledges the important influence CONSER has on the application of serials cataloging policy, "that CONSER is not a world unto itself and therefore must coordinate its efforts with other relevant groups."[5] Indeed, since then, CONSER has proven to be capable of setting and documenting quality standards for serials cataloging as well as delivering a reliable database constructed in accordance with these. While there will undoubtedly be value to the role an established cooperative cataloging program can play in setting standards for cataloging digital resources, the CONSER model will be tested in terms of its flexibility. With some issues related to digital resources and serials, for example, CONSER policy may have to be easily and quickly changed. Some issues may, in fact, benefit from experimentation and testing before standards and policy are permanently set.

The mechanisms for communication provided through e-mail, listservs (SERIALST, CONSRLST and CONSERline), and Web pages facilitate a more interactive and dynamic program structure. Even if we don't keep the network lines humming each day with CONSER activity, we know it is an option whenever an issue needs debating or airing. This, in fact, was the strategy taken for drafting policy on a number of the issues related to electronic serials in developing CCM Module 31.[6] So long as the CONSER members remain committed to the kind of continual program assessment that will keep it in line with institutional priorities, the members can adapt the program to be as vibrant as it needs to be through a period of very changeable and dynamic publication patterns. In his article on "Symmetry and Extrapolation: Passion and Precision–Cooperative Cataloging at the Beginning of the 21st Century," Greg Anderson claims that CONSER participants are able to bring both passion and precision to their work. He notes that "it is only when equality and latitude are recognized for everyone that passion and precision can prosper. The interesting theme here is caring; caring by everyone about the database–the centerpiece of the entire enterprise, caring about participation, about equality and a level playing field for all participants."[7]

REFERENCES

1. O'Neil, Rosanna M., "CONSER: Cons . . . and Pros, or What's in it for me?" *Serials Review*, Summer 1991, pp. 53-62.

2. Anderson, Bill, "History of the CONSER Program, 1986-1994," *Serials Review*, v. 21, no. 2, Summer 1995, p. 9.

3. Cole, Jim E. and Madison, Olivia M. A., "A Decade of Serials Cataloging," *The Serials Librarian*, v. 10, Fall 1985-Winter 1986, p. 114.

4. Barron, Lucy A. and Bartley, Linda K., "Concerning CONSER: Accomplishments and Aspirations," *The Serials Librarian*, v. 19, no. 3-4, 1991, p. 179.

5. Bartley, Linda K. and Reynolds, Regina R., "CONSER: Revolution and Evolution," *Cataloging & Classification Quarterly.* v. 8, no. 3-4, p. 63.

6. Anderson, Bill, *Serials Review*, p. 10.

7. Anderson, Greg, "Symmetry and Extrapolation: Passion and Precision–Cooperative Cataloging at the Beginning of the 21st Century," *Cataloging & Classification Quarterly*, v. 17, no. 3-4, 1993, p. 57.

A Client-Server Serials Control System for Staff and Public Access Functions

Mary C. Schlembach
William H. Mischo

SUMMARY. This paper describes a networked serials control system developed at the Grainger Engineering Library Information Center at the University of Illinois at Urbana-Champaign (UIUC). The Grainger serials control system encompasses serials processing, public service, and end-user functions. The system employs a client-server computing architecture with a microcomputer client written in Visual Basic accessing a networked SQL relational database. The Grainger serials control system is designed to: expedite check-in, binding, and claiming within a graphical user interface; provide expanded search capabilities and access points; provide a Notes capability for public service staff; provide a user-friendly interface for patrons; and serve as a testbed for interface design and database techniques applied to serials control systems, and by extension to other search and retrieval systems. *[Article copies available for a fee from The Haworth Document Delivery Service: 1-800-342-9678. E-mail address: getinfo@haworth.com]*

Numerous articles have described automated serials control systems and detailed the evolving features and functions of these sys-

---

Mary C. Schlembach is Assistant Engineering Librarian, and William H. Mischo is Engineering Librarian, both at the Grainger Engineering Library Information Center, University of Illinois at Urbana-Champaign, 1301 W. Springfield Avenue, Urbana, IL 61801.

[Haworth co-indexing entry note]: "A Client-Server Serials Control System for Staff and Public Access Functions." Schlembach, Mary C., and William H. Mischo. Co-published simultaneously in *The Serials Librarian* (The Haworth Press, Inc.) Vol. 29, No. 3/4, 1996, pp. 113-140; and: *Serials Management in the Electronic Era: Papers in Honor of Peter Gellatly, Founding Editor of* The Serials Librarian (ed: Jim Cole, and James W. Williams) The Haworth Press, Inc., 1996, pp. 113-140. Single or multiple copies of this article are available for a fee from The Haworth Document Delivery Service [1-800-342-9678, 9:00 a.m. - 5:00 p.m. (EST). E-mail address: getinfo@haworth.com].

113

tems.[1-5] Methodologies and procedures for the design of a serials control system have been described by Hannah.[6] In the last several years, with the availability of powerful personal computer workstations and local and wide-area networked computing environments, a number of microcomputer-based serials control systems have been introduced.[7-8] This article reports on a serials control system developed at the Grainger Engineering Library Information Center at the University of Illinois at Urbana-Champaign that is based on client-server technologies in a Windows/Novell/TCP/IP environment. This system employs a microcomputer client with a graphical user interface written in Visual Basic that accesses a networked SQL (Structured Query Language) relational database residing on a Microsoft Access or Microsoft SQL Server database management system.

The Grainger serials control system is designed to meet the following goals:

1. to expedite check-in, binding, claiming, and routing operations for the Grainger serials collection;
2. to provide expanded search capabilities and access points to the Grainger serials collection (not only for titles currently received but also for ceased, closed and changed titles);
3. to provide distributed multi-user access to serial check-in, holdings, and binding information for Grainger and other departmental library staff at public service points scattered throughout the building and from other departmental libraries;
4. to allow public service staff to enter and save comments at the record level in a Notes field;
5. to provide patrons at public terminals, via a user-friendly interface, with keyword and subject access to serials holding information and links to journal tables of contents;
6. to design a system using off-the-shelf software components that will accommodate other serial publications, such as government publications and monographic series;
7. to provide a rapid development software testbed that can be used to test interface design and database techniques applied to serials control systems, and, by extension, to other bibliographic retrieval systems.

This paper will describe the features of the Grainger serials control system and provide several accompanying screen images to illustrate important details.

The UIUC Library system is comprised of central Acquisitions and Serials Departments and 38 departmental libraries, all of which, to some extent, directly receive periodical subscription issues. While the UIUC Library has recently begun implementation of the Innovac serials control module, the system is being used for centrally received periodicals.

The Grainger Engineering Library Information Center, which opened in 1994, currently directly receives approximately 1300 periodical titles. The Grainger facility has separate circulation and reference desks, two entrances/exits, a current periodicals room, and a staff work area–all of which are physically separated from each other. One of the primary design requirements for the new facility was to provide fast, convenient access to serials information from these separate service desks, public points, and staff areas. Distance and security concerns precluded staff and patrons, particularly after regular business hours, from entering the technical processing areas where the manual serials check-in Kardex system was located.

Grainger Engineering Library staff designed and developed a serials control system that attempts to address the specified goals outlined above. The Grainger computing environment is comprised of staff and public PCs attached to both a Novell local area network and a TCP/IP campus wide-area network. The serials control system operates in a client-server environment with a central database accessible from staff PCs, reference and circulation desk workstations, and public library terminals. The system is comprised of client software written in Visual Basic 3.0, which provides a search and display interface and establishes connections to networked Microsoft Access and Microsoft SQL server databases containing the central database. There is a staff version of the client which provides check-in and add/delete records to authorized staff. The staff version includes search and annotation functions for public service staff. A public terminal version of the client provides end-user searching and browsing of the serials system. The database is capable of being dynamically updated from the staff client by authorized users. System features used in conjunction with check-in, reference, and patron searching are described below. The software suite can be modified to accommodate other types of serial publications requiring indexing, check-in, holdings, and expanded searching capabilities.

DATABASE DESIGN

While the term "client-server" has been variously defined, we will use client-server here to define a networked computing environment with client PCs responsible for interface, display, query, and database updating functions operating on a dynamic master database residing on a file server, usually a special-purpose PC or UNIX platform. The client software presents the user with interface software that controls the fetching and displaying of database information, and initiates changes in the database based on user input.

The Serials Control database uses off-the-shelf microcomputer and server software, employing the Microsoft Access and Microsoft SQL server relational database management software with front-end software written in Visual Basic 3.0. Microsoft Access and SQL Server use a relational database model, with data residing in data tables containing discrete records comprised of separate fields. The tables are related or linked by common keys or index entries. The Grainger Serials database originally resided on a Microsoft Access database and was accessed over a Novell local-area network. The database has since been migrated to a Microsoft SQL Server database residing on a Windows NT server and accessed using the TCP/IP protocol.

In our Serials database construct, the Access table FullRec contains fields containing the data for the display, the check-in operation and binding information for each record (Figure 1). Other information used for search and display is contained in the Subject Headings, Title, Unique Words and Unique Subjects tables (Figure 2). The link key for all the relational tables is the Call Number field. Several term occurrence tables are linked to heading tables that are, in turn, linked by call number to the FullRec table for final retrieval and display. For example, the Unique Subject Table (Figure 3)

FIGURE 1. Full Record Table

Field Name:	Value:
TITLE:	Systems & Control Letters
CALLNO:	ENX 001.6105SYC
ISSN:	0167-6911
FAXONNO:	11- 1191
VENDOR:	Blackwell
FREQUENCY:	m
CHECKIN:	v. 18, no. 1, 1992 JAN 08-13-199
BINDING:	v. 20, no. 1, 1993 JAN 08-13-199
NEXTEXP:	1995-12-23
LASTVOL:	26
LASTISS:	3
LASTYR:	1995
LASTMONTH:	9
TABCON:	2
NOTES:	
TITLEKEY:	Systems Control Letters
NOTES2:	
PRICE:	576
ACCESSION:	10

Window title bar: K:\MATPROC\SERIAL.MDB : FULLREC
Buttons: Add | Update | Delete | Find | Refresh

provides an alphabetical listing of headings with the number of occurrences of each heading. The headings provide a link to the Subject Heading Table, which lists each heading and the associated call numbers in the FullRec table. When patrons search for a subject heading, they retrieve the number of occurrences of the heading, which then links each occurrence to its associated full record. In the same manner, the Unique Words Table (Figure 4) contains an alpha-

FIGURE 2. Tables used for searching and browsing subject headings, unique words and titles.

⊟	K:\MATPROC\SERIAL.MDB : SUBJHEAD				▼	▲
Add	Update	Delete	Find	Refresh		
Field Name:	**Value:**					
CALLNO:	ENX 001.6105SYC					
HEADING:	Control theory					
◄ ◄ Editing Record					► ►►	

⊟	K:\MATPROC\SERIAL.MDB : TITLE				▼	▲
Add	Update	Delete	Find	Refresh		
Field Name:	**Value:**					
TITLEF:	Systems & Control Letters					
CALLNO:	ENX 001.6105SYC					
◄ ◄ Editing Record					► ►►	

⊟	K:\MATPROC\SERIAL.MDB : UNIQWORDS				▼	·
Add	Update	Delete	Find	Refresh		
Field Name:	**Value:**					
WORD:	System					
OCCS:	5					
◄ ◄ Editing Record					►	

⊟	K:\MATPROC\SERIAL.MDB : UNIQUESUBJ				▼	▲
Add	Update	Delete	Find	Refresh		
Field Name:	**Value:**					
HEADING:	Control theory					
OCCS:	9					
◄ ◄ Editing Record					► ►	

FIGURE 3. Unique Subject Heading Table. This table links the occurrences of subject headings to the Subject Headings Table, which then links to the full record by call number.

⊟	K:\MATPROC\SERIAL.MDB : UNIQUESUBJ				
Add	Update	Delete	Find	Refresh	
Field Name:	**Value:**				
HEADING:	Control theory				
OCCS:	9				

FIGURE 4. Unique Words Table. Counts the number of times specific words appear in database.

▭	K:\MATPROC\SERIAL.MDB: UNIQWORDS			
Add	Update	Delete	Find	Refresh

Field Name: Value:

WORD: Control

OCCS: 41

betical listing of individual title and subject words and the number of times the words occur in the records. The word lists, or "word wheels," are also used by staff and patrons as a spelling aid in Browse mode to facilitate title and subject retrieval. While the unique key for the FullRec table in the database is the call number, the entire database can be sorted and displayed by any searchable field: call number, title, ISSN, vendor, Faxon number, Next Expected Date, and Frequency (Figure 5).

To automate and expedite the check-in function better, the database design includes fields in each record for frequency of publication, last volume number received, last issue number received, year of last issue, and last month (1 through 12) received. These fields are used to calculate the volume, issue number, and year of the next expected issue (see below under Check-In section) and provide single click check-in.

The Grainger Serials database utilizes a relational database structure that allows the interface software to query the database using SQL commands. SQL (pronounced "sequel") is a standard query language employed in relational databases. It uses a powerful and extendable search syntax to retrieve sets of records from database tables.[9] For example, the SQL command to retrieve all the matching records with the title phrase "IEEE Quantum" would be *Select * from FullRec where TitleKey like '*IEEE*Quantum*' order by CallNo.* This command would look at the FullRec table and retrieve all matches with both "IEEE" and "Quantum" within the TitleKey field, allowing words to appear before "IEEE," after "Quantum," and between the two words. The matching records, or hits, are returned in call number order. In our implementation, the SQL

FIGURE 5. Database Sort Pull-Down Menu Options

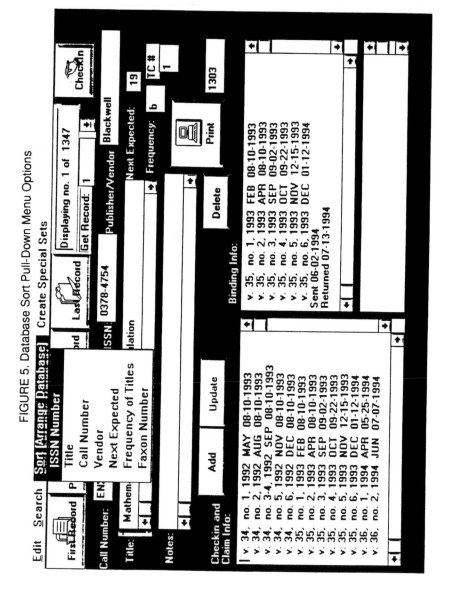

commands are all formulated by the interface software from user-entered search terms. The search language syntax, semantics, and truncation symbols of SQL are completely shielded from the user.

The serials control system provides check-in and binding functions and includes the capability of adding new titles to the database and deleting records for serials that are withdrawn. The entire record, with all user-changeable fields, is displayed on a single screen for easy updating (Figure 6). Therefore, all fields can be dynamically updated by authorized staff directly on the screen. Changes made by staff on screen fields are copied into the database at the record level either when the next record is displayed, or a new search is instituted, or the record is otherwise refreshed, such as at the logoff stage. The software design allows changing the search options and linking the display text boxes to other defined fields in a relational database. The flexibility of this design makes the database extremely generic and allows modifications in the structure to accommodate different types of data.

While the Serials database is not in MARC format, it can be easily converted to MARC format at output. Indeed, the database was initially constructed from MARC format records. Likewise, the Grainger Serials Control system does not use the U.S. MARC Format for Holdings and Locations standard, but the text is in a field-delimited format that allows output and conversion to any desired standard format.

SEARCH CAPABILITIES

The system features a rich set of search options to optimize retrieval for technical services staff, public service staff, and patrons. The Search options are displayed in Figure 7. They include: the capability to search title keywords or title left-hand matches and to search for either first matching hit or the set of all matches; Call number; ISSN (first matching or all); Keywords within Check-in, Notes, Binding; Faxon number, and Next Expected Date. It is important to note that all of the fields can be searched using both left-hand and right-hand truncation or stemming. This is a built-in feature of SQL.

The Serials Control record display form includes buttons for

FIGURE 6. Serials Control Interface

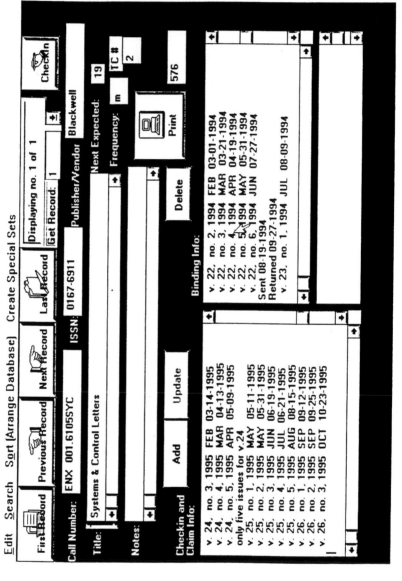

FIGURE 7. Search Pull-Down Menu Options/Title Search Options

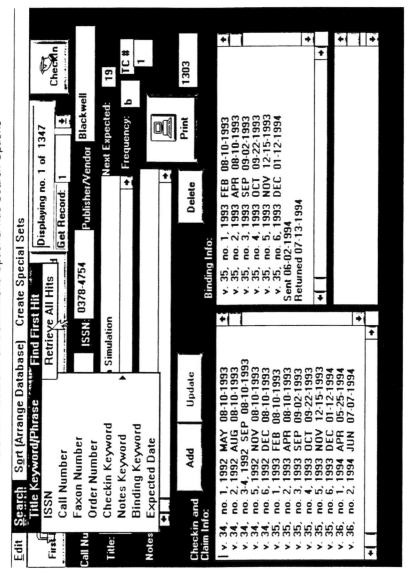

123

advancing to Next or Previous record, or to jump to the First or Last record in the retrieved set. In addition, a particular record can be displayed by typing in the desired record number in the Displayed Record box. The form contains title, call number, scrollable text boxes that display all Check-in and Claim information, Binding information, Next Expected Issue, Frequency, ISSN, Vendor, number of Tables of Contents to be routed to faculty, names and addresses for Table of Contents routing, and a Notes section where staff are able to save notes indicating special instructions, comments or procedures for a particular title. The form also includes a Print button, and for authorized technical processing staff, Check-in, Add Record, and Delete Record buttons (Figure 6). The displayed text boxes are linked, or bound, to the database and changes can be made to the database (by authorized staff) in real-time by entering or deleting text in the appropriate boxes.

The serials control system also allows for the search and display of Special Sets generated by predefined search strategies. These Sets include: all items sent to the bindery, all titles with outstanding claims, all titles with missing issues or replacements ordered, all issues expected by today or this month, all order records, and all titles with attached notes placed by either technical processing staff, public service staff, or patrons (Figure 8). These Special Sets can be browsed online, downloaded, or printed.

SERIALS PROCESSING

Check-In

The check-in module is designed to facilitate the check-in process. To accomplish this, the module supports the following features:

- a graphical user interface containing command buttons and list boxes;
- database fields storing the next expected volume, issue number, month, and year for each title;
- a one-click check-in of the next predicted issue;
- the ability to increment by one the volume, issue, and year before a one-click check-in of the issue;

- one-click recording of the receipt of duplicate and/or supplemental issues (our convention is to use an asterisk behind the issue number);
- check-in dates that are automatically generated by the software based on the computer system's internal calendar; and
- automatic calculation of the date of the next expected issue based on the date of check-in and the frequency of the title.

In order to insure that only designated members of the staff have check-in capability, a password screen has been created (Figure 9).

Every periodical title is assigned one of the following frequency codes: d = daily, w = weekly, m = monthly, b = bi-monthly, q = quarterly, s = semi-annually, a = annual or i = irregular. The frequency code and last checked-in date are used to predict automatically the date when the next issue is expected to arrive. Check-in is designed to be accomplished, in most cases, with one click of a button.

As journals are received for check-in, the journal titles are typically searched by ISSN, title, or call number through the database client. Barcode searching is not presently supported since the UIUC library circulation system does not currently use barcoding.

Since the next expected issue has been calculated for the staff member by the system, it requires only a quick visual check to see if the issue matches (Figure 10). If an issue has been skipped, the missing issue information can be recorded in the check-in information field. The claim process, which at UIUC is a manual process requiring filling out a form and sending to the central acquisitions department, can then be instituted. This provides a mechanism for searching and browsing for unreceived claimed issues on a regular basis, or as desired. The serials information display provides convenient access to vendor and claim information.

Upon receipt of the first number of a new volume, the system displays a message to the staff member indicating a potential binding situation with the option to print a reminder notice to pick up the title for binding.

FIGURE 8. Create Special Sets Pull-Down Menu Options

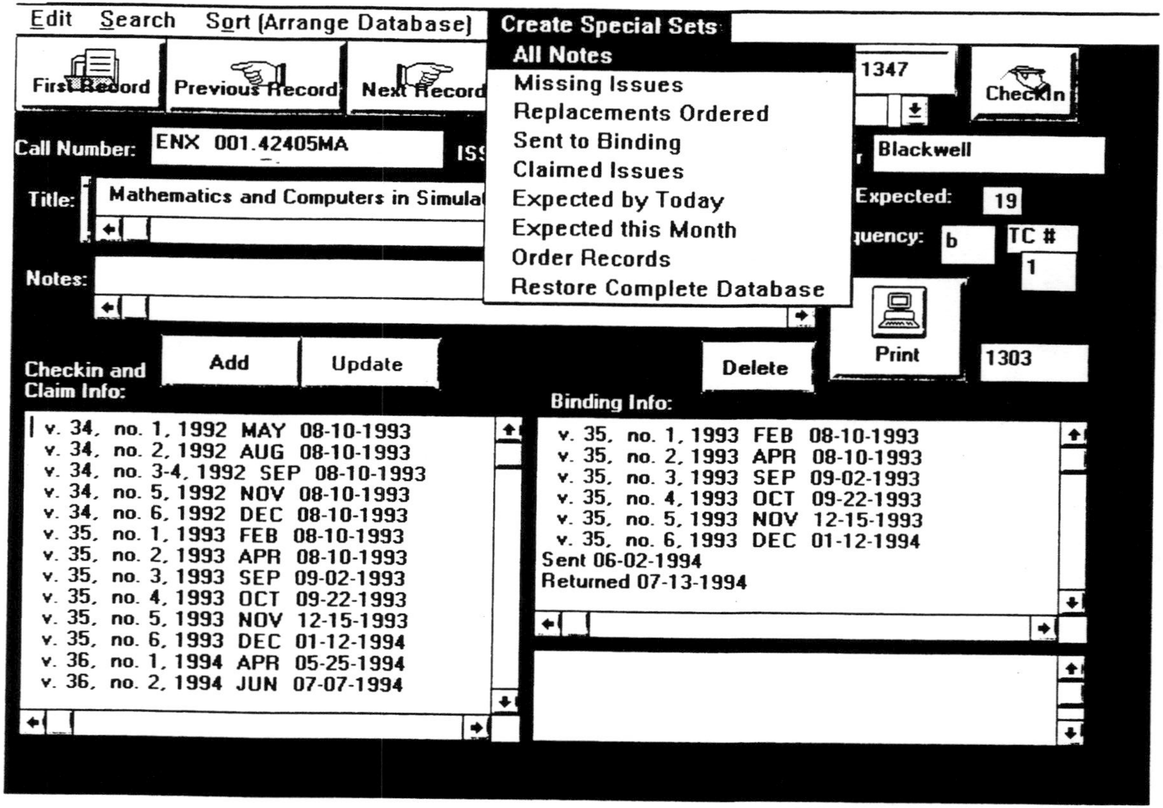

FIGURE 9. Password Interface

Binding

Binding Information is recorded in a separate field that includes volume and issues sent to the bindery with the date sent and, subsequently, the date returned.

Sending journals to binding is as simple as highlighting the desired block of issues, copying to the clipboard (via a "copy-and-paste" operation using Control keys or picking "Copy" and "Paste" from the Windows menu "Edit" options), and clicking on the desired location in the binding field. The phrase "Sent Out" and the day's date is added at the bottom of the set with a function key. When the bound volumes are returned, staff simply place the cursor at the bottom of the "Sent Out" section and press a function key.

FIGURE 10. Check-In Interface

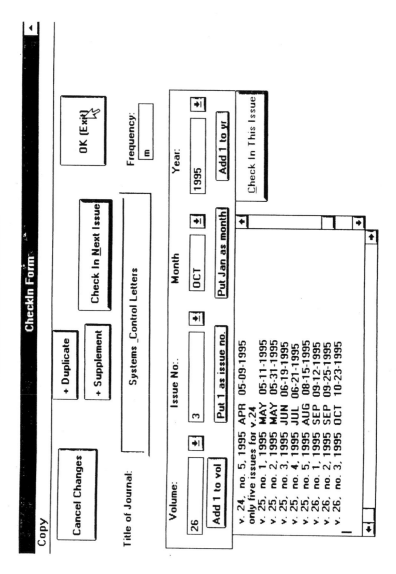

The phrase "Returned" and the current date are added to the text box and "Sent Out" is programmatically changed to "Sent."

Print Options

All search results can be printed with the assistance of a Print form that allows the user to choose from a number of printing options (Figure 11). Call numbers and titles are the default on all printouts. Multiple check boxes allow the user to add to the default print options of title and call number and choose, in addition, the vendor, price, ISSN, Frequency, Last Volume or Issue received, Next Expected, Bindery "Sent Out" dates, Claimed Issues, Price, and Subject Headings. Printing options allow printing of a single item, a range of records, or all records that have a search set result of 100 or fewer titles. Each printed page has a header and page number and can also contain a user-supplied header.

PUBLIC SERVICE USAGE/USE

Several authors have described the public service implications of making available current serials holding and binding information.[10-11] While providing this information will place burdens on public service staff, the value of making this important information available, particularly in a science and engineering collection, far outweighs the inconveniences. The Grainger serials control system has been used extensively for the last several years at public service points to assist users with periodical availability and holding questions.

Public service staff are able to enter free-text information into the Notes field. This information might indicate a patron's inability to locate an issue, or to alert the processing staff to notify patrons or other staff upon receipt of the next issue(s). All Notes are searchable and messages are followed-up on by serials staff.

The expanded search capabilities, in particular the capability to search by keyword over title and corporate authors, have proven valuable to public service staff attempting to verify an inaccurate citation. Keyword searching in the check-in field has also proven to

FIGURE 11. Print Interface

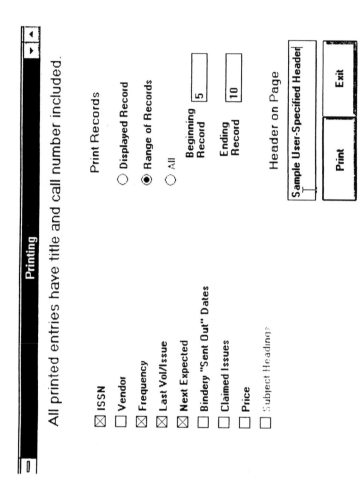

be useful. For example, patrons often approach the reference desk with a citation in which the title is incorrect but the volume number is correct or vice-versa. These citations can often be verified with a keyword search for volume number in the check-in field.

The Binding fields are invaluable to Reference staff who are frequently asked why an issue is not on the shelf. The dates provide an idea as to when it will return from the bindery. Patrons anxiously awaiting a particular issue can determine when it is expected to return and have a "notify" placed on the record Notes field for them by public service staff. Because the binding information is not presently being erased, the binding field also indicates to staff information concerning bound volumes, and complements information in the circulation system.

In addition, the user can access a separate, comprehensive Grainger Library serial database consisting of over 5,000 active, canceled, ceased or changed titles representing all the titles that have ever been received at the Library. This database also includes some continuation titles and monographic series. This larger database is used to generate a printed Journal List (Figure 12). Updating these databases is straightforward since most multiple title searches find cross-references, title changes, and absorptions.

In addition to the efficiency that the Serial Control system provides to the technical staff, it can also be used for other serial-type publications. We have used the same database model in creating a database for Patent and Trademark Abstracts (Figure 13). We have also adapted the database model and generic search engine to produce systems to access the Reserves collection, the Reference collection, a faculty interest file, a new-books database, and a number of customized databases, such as the IEEE holdings list.

Public Access Version

The Grainger Library has created a public access client for the Serials Control system, which provides searching over the same database and using the same access capabilities. The public access version is being made available at public terminals using a specially designed search interface that supports a number of search and browse options.

FIGURE 12. Journal List

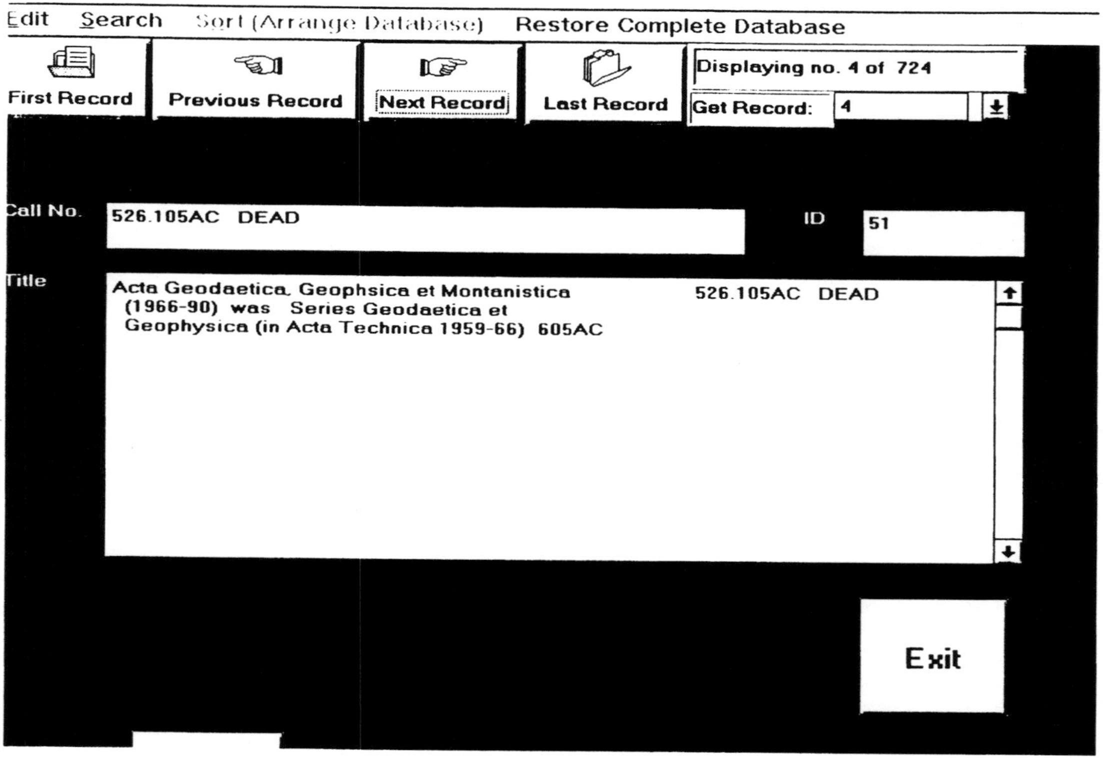

FIGURE 13. Patents and Trademark Database

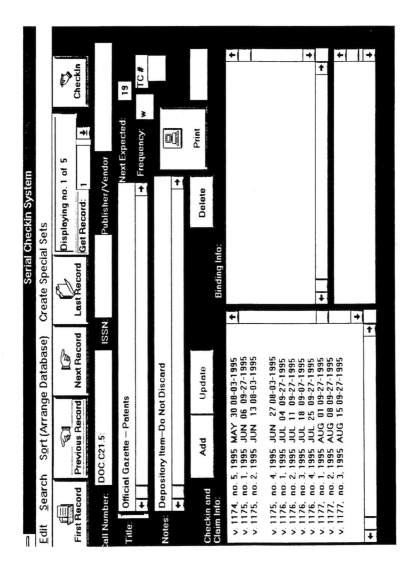

The search features include:

- Title keyword, title left hand match (with truncation), and exact title (Figure 14);
- Call number partial match (to retrieve all partial call numbers, such as 621.3);
- Subject keyword and subject left hand match (with truncation).

The system provides automatic left and right hand truncation to user-entered search arguments. One interesting feature of the retrieval software is the capability to modify the search after the system returns the initial number of hits or matches. With the click of a button, users can redo the search with the last letter of the search argument removed or browse a list of words/phrases alphabetically close to their entered search argument. This addresses user spelling errors, allows selection of multiple terms to be ORed or ANDed together in a search argument, and greatly enhances retrieval capability.

The browse functions provide users with alphabetically displayed lists of terms along with their total occurrences in the database. The browse options include:

- Title words;
- Full titles;
- Subject headings (Figure 15).

The browse software allows the selection of multiple term entries (along with their attached database occurrences) from the browse list for retrieval and display. These selected items can be searched as exact matches or word/phrase stems and combined using either an OR or an AND operator.

This public version accesses the same Serials database and is available from public terminal PCs throughout the building. On the public version, all fields are display only, with a provision to leave suggestions or comments in a separate, editable field.

From the public version client, users can display check-in and binding information for retrieved titles. Users can also retrieve titles received in the last week (Figure 16). In addition, location information for specific call numbers can be brought up in a display form (Figure 17). More detailed links to the library floor-plans are being designed, to further assist patrons in finding journals.

FIGURE 14. Public Access Search Options/Title Options

Grainger Engineering Library Information Center

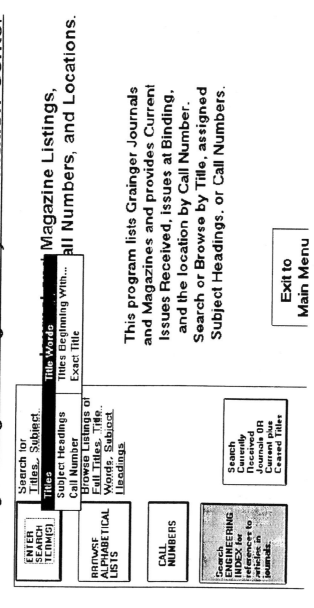

FIGURE 15. Subject Heading Browse Interface

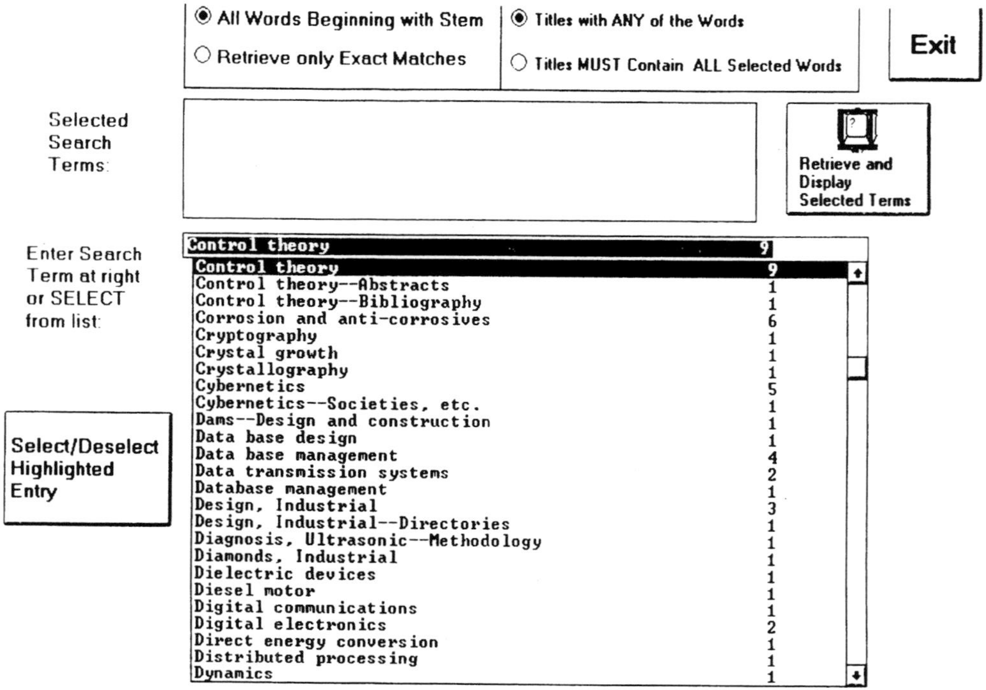

FIGURE 16. Public Access Recently Received Interface

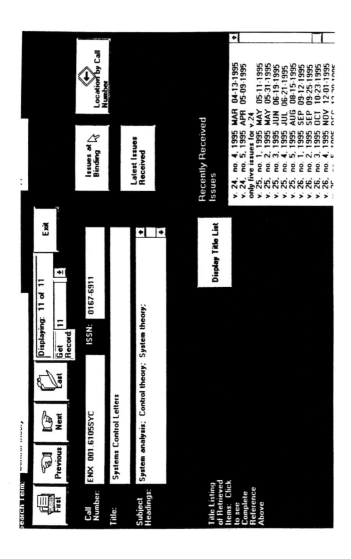

FIGURE 17. Call Number Locations

Call Number Locations

All journals received in the past 3 years are located in the Current Periodicals Room located on the First Floor – West side – in alphabetical order by Title. Previous issues are located by Call Number in the following locations:

Call Number of Current Item: ENX 001.6105SYC

001 – 530.999	Third Floor, East
531 – 613.999	Second Floor, East
614 – 621.999	Third Floor, West
621.3 – 621.799	Second Floor, West
621.8 – 628.999	Lower Level, Center
629 – End	Lower Level, West

Exit

The public client main menu provides access to a locally mounted Compendex (Engineering Index) database for access to the journal literature at the article level. With the use of optical character recognition (OCR) scanners, we will be experimenting with providing scanned tables of contents for selected journals to allow users to browse the tables of contents of recently received journals.

Printing options for the public service version also have a title and call number default. It also allows users to print their own specified header on each page with options for a single record, range of records, or all records in a search result of 25 or fewer titles.

(Readers interested in receiving a Microsoft Access blank database template of this software should contact Mary C. Schlembach at Grainger Engineering Library Information Center, 1301 West Springfield Avenue, Urbana, IL 61801 or e-mail schlemba@uiuc.edu.)

NOTES

1. Trisha Davis, *Serials Control Systems for Libraries,* Westport, CT: Mecklermedia, 1994.

2. Richard W. Boss, "Developing Requirements for Automated Serials Control Systems," NASIG Proceedings, *The Serials Librarian* 11 (Dec. 86/Jan. 87): 37-71.

3. Ronald A. Gardner, "The Evolution of Automated Serials Control," *The Serials Librarian* 11 (Dec. 86/Jan. 87):71-83.

4. James E. Rush, "Automated Serials Control Systems," *Serials Review* 12, (Summer/Fall 1986):87-101.

5. Carol Pitts Hawks, "Automated Library Systems: What Next?" Plenary Session 3 Strategies and Responses, *The Serials Librarian* 21, nos. 2-3 (1991):87-96.

6. Stanley A. Hannah, "A Comparison of Software Methodologies in the Development of a Serials Control System." PhD Thesis, Indiana University, 1994.

7. Mary Anne Royle, "Serials Control with Microcomputers in the Law Library: Choices and Challenges," *The Serials Librarian* 13 (Sept. 1987):11-19.

8. Kenneth L. Kirkland, "Methods and Madness to Migration to Micros (three presentations which described movement to microcomputer serial control systems," *The Serials Librarian* 13), (Oct/Nov. 1987): 149-154.

9. Jeff Prosise, "Guide to Computer Acronyms, Part 2." *PC Magazine* 15, (Jan. 23, 1996): 211-217.

10. Roger L. Presley, "The Goldfish Bowl Effect of an Online Serials Control System" *The Serials Librarian* 11, (Dec. 86/Jan. 87): 101-9.

11. Laura Peritore, "Public access to serials check-in information and its impact on reference services (at 3 university libraries)" *Reference Librarian* 27-28, (1989): 17-37.

Electronic "Keyboard Pals": Mentoring the Electronic Way

Kathryn Luther Henderson

SUMMARY. In the spring semester 1995 offering of the Technical Services Functions course (LIS 437) at the Graduate School of Library and Information Science, University of Illinois at Urbana-Champaign, each student was assigned two practicing technical services librarians to serve as electronic mail mentors. The mentors were available throughout the semester primarily to serve as resource persons for a major course paper. They also provided counsel and guidance related to other aspects of the course's content. Evaluations by both mentors and "mentees" indicated that this was a successful use of this new means of communication. *[Article copies available for a fee from The Haworth Document Delivery Service: 1-800-342-9678. E-mail address: getinfo@ haworth.com]*

INTRODUCTION

It is no secret that increasingly librarians depend on electronic communications for their daily work. One means of this communicating is by electronic mail (e-mail) which is used by technical services librarians in a variety of ways from internal memos to consultation with a serials vendor halfway around the world.

Kathryn Luther Henderson is Professor, Graduate School of Library and Information Science, University of Illinois at Urbana-Champaign, 501 E. Daniel Street, Champaign, IL 61820-6211 (E-mail: henderso@alexia.lis.uiuc.edu).

[Haworth co-indexing entry note]: "Electronic 'Keyboard Pals': Mentoring the Electronic Way." Henderson, Kathryn Luther. Co-published simultaneously in *The Serials Librarian* (The Haworth Press, Inc.) Vol. 29, No. 3/4, 1996, pp. 141-164; and: *Serials Management in the Electronic Era: Papers in Honor of Peter Gellatly, Founding Editor of* The Serials Librarian (ed: Jim Cole, and James W. Williams) The Haworth Press, Inc., 1996, pp. 141-164. Single or multiple copies of this article are available for a fee from The Haworth Document Delivery Service [1-800-342-9678, 9:00 a.m. - 5:00 p.m. (EST). E-mail address: getinfo@haworth.com].

Communication does not always come easy even in the speedy world of e-mail which, on the surface, tends to be more informal than that found in a formal business letter. Students in today's schools of library and information science must learn to engage in this newer form of communication along with learning how to frame the questions and comments for interaction with colleagues and business associates in whatever form communication may occur. Several schools are engaged in experiments in the use of electronic means of communication. Several efforts at the Graduate School of Library and Information Science (GSLIS), University of Illinois at Urbana-Champaign (UIUC) have matched up students who are enrolled in similar courses in other schools. In fall 1994, this writer envisioned taking a different approach—matching, through e-mail, practicing technical services librarians as mentors with students in the spring 1995 Technical Services Functions course (LIS 437). As this idea began to take shape, a mentor began to be thought of as a resource person for several students. Serving throughout the semester, the mentor would specifically assist the students by answering questions and making comments that related to a required paper for the course. In effect, a mentor would serve as a professional helping to guide future professionals through an understanding of the issues raised in the course or raised by the student or mentor. That a personal link between generations might be formed was also an important objective of the project.

Since there was sparse documentation of previous attempts for this specific type of mentoring,[1] the instructor explored the idea with colleagues at GSLIS and with Dean Leigh Estabrook. Because cooperation with practicing librarians would be a necessity, e-mail messages of inquiry were sent to a few technical services librarians who were known to have Internet access and who were likely to give the instructor honest feedback concerning the idea. Reply, they did—with enthusiasm. Who could dare *not* go through with an idea that received responses such as:

- "It sounds like an excellent idea to me. It sounds like the kind of draft/revision process that happens in the 'real world' all the time. And I will probably get as much, if not more, out of it as the students do. I look forward to it."

- "I would be delighted to do. What a splendid idea."
- "It sounds like it would be rewarding, educational and fun."
- "Sounds like a good idea to me . . . I have found contacts in other libraries to be very valuable. . . . Getting your students started communicating this way is one of the most important things you can teach them, in my opinion."
- "I would love to be a mentor."
- "That's an excellent idea . . . thank you for thinking of me."
- "This sounds like fun, and not a lot of work. At least I won't be writing the paper! There could even be some issues my traditional catalogers could use some help [in seeing in a new] light from the perspective of idealistic library school students. Count me in!"

THE COURSE

Technical Services Functions (LIS 437) was established as a one unit (i.e., four credit hour) graduate level course at GSLIS in 1981. Ironically, this was at a time when the future of technical services as a formal division in libraries was being questioned. With the exception of one year, when the instructor was on sabbatical leave, this elective course has been offered every spring semester and usually attracts the limit, set by the instructor, of 20-25 students. Many of the students do not necessarily expect to work as technical services librarians but, regardless of their career paths, realize the importance of knowing about the functions of technical services.

The areas covered in the course have always included technical services in general, preservation, acquisitions, and serials control and management. (LIS 437 is one of the few courses in the curriculum to cover serials in any depth.) As some aspects of technical and public services have tended to merge, access services is a topic now covered allowing for discussion, for example, of the relationship of document delivery to serials management. Cataloging is covered in other courses but serials cataloging is a component of LIS 437.

Extensive course syllabi are included with each unit. Annotated bibliographies are updated for each offering of the course. Students report wide use of these sources not only in the course but also as a part of their own continuing education programs after graduation.

In-class conduct of the course is essentially as a seminar course with students heavily involved in participation in each session. Practicing technical services librarians often add their expertise to some of the sessions either by their presence or through the submission of ideas and materials to the instructor. The students are supplied with vendor catalogs and two representatives from vendor communities come to particular sessions. One of these vendors always represents serials.

Various papers or problems are a part of the course and a term project is the student's attempt at synthesis. Students choose their project, write a proposal to be commented on by the instructor, complete the project, and give a brief report to the entire class at the time set for the final examination. Many interesting projects emerge such as "shadowing" a technical services librarian for a specified period of time; outlining a disaster preparedness plan; determining ergonomic features in furnishings and equipment for technical services work; discussing collection development issues; considering the changing roles of professional and paraprofessional cataloging staff; evaluating automated serials control systems; performing serials cataloging, etc.

In the 1995 offering, the students had access to an electronic bulletin board for the class available through the School's LAN. Here the students and the instructor posted notices relevant to the course's content. The students were informed about various listservs that related to the course and addresses for subscribing to them were included in the syllabus for each unit; however, in the interest of saving overall disk space in the local system, the instructor most often forwarded her "copies" of the following subscriptions or excerpts from them to the LIS 437 electronic bulletin board: *ALCTS Network News*; *ACQNET*; *SERIALST*; and *Newsletter on Serials Pricing Issues*. A student from a preservation course of the previous semester forwarded relevant *Conservation DistList* postings. The instructor often issued her own commentaries about the topics discussed in the postings or related them to other aspects of the course. Here was a way, in addition to readings, visits, and class discussion, to relate the students' course work to the "real world." The electronic means is particularly important for bringing students up-to-date on volatile issues such as serials pricing.

BACK TO MENTORING

A decision was made that each student would have two mentors and each mentor would work with one or two students. Before registration, one could not with exactness know the course enrollment; however, knowing the usual number of students who enroll and the top limits set by the instructor allowed for preliminary inquiries to be made to potential mentors. Mentors were to be matched as closely as possible to interests of the students—for example, those specifically interested in serials cataloging with serials catalogers; those with preservation interests with preservation librarians; etc. As far as possible, a student would also be paired with a mentor who was working in a type of library in which the student was especially interested. As the class makeup emerged, it was apparent that an unusually large number of students interested in public librarianship had enrolled. Finding participants working in technical services in public libraries with e-mail addresses proved not to be an easy task. The same was true for the one student interested in theological librarianship; in this instance, we resorted to the use of telephone, surface mail and an actual visit by the student to a Chicago theological seminary.

Except for one person, all mentors were graduates of GSLIS and all graduates had been students of the present instructor, if not in this particular course, then in cataloging or preservation courses. Eleven of the 26 had themselves been students in previous Technical Services Functions offerings. The length of time spent in technical services work of the mentors varied among the former GSLIS students from one to almost thirty years.

Requirements for choosing mentors were:

1. e-mail addresses known to the instructor
2. engaged in technical services work or close relationship to technical services work (e.g., systems librarian)
3. willingness to fully participate throughout the semester.

It was clearly NOT a random sample!

In November and December 1994, e-mail messages were sent to most of the potential mentors. (A few more addresses became known later and additional mentors were added as course enrollment stabilized.) An explanation was given concerning expectations of the mentors including an estimate of the amount of time required. They were sent a copy of the assignment around which the main mentoring project would be oriented.

With e-mail speed, positive replies similar to the initial sample inquiries were received. Only two persons declined the invitation—one because of installation of a new system that was underway in her library which would keep her very busy in the timeframe of the project; the other because of a supervisor's reluctance to sanction participation.

Mentors were sent brief informational statements about their students and students were given a similar short introduction to their mentors. Mentor and "mentee" were asked early on to introduce him/herself to the other.

THE ASSIGNMENT
"Technical Services: A Think Piece"

The assignment was to be an ongoing one, the written component of which was to be completed by no later than April 11, 1995, three months into the semester after many of the units in the course had been covered. This assignment would comprise 25% of the course grade and came to be referred to as the "Think Piece."

The purpose of the study was described as follows:

> to provide something of "an integrated whole" covering various aspects of technical services. Here you will wrestle with some of the main issues of technical services, with conflicting ideas, with old and new tensions. Soon you will be in the midst of the "real" world, called upon to confront the issues and take a "stand." And perhaps even resolve some of the tensions. Here is your opportunity to read about, discuss and confront the tensions, and come to some of your own decisions while also allowing room to air some of your doubts and anxieties.

The requirements of the assignment were described thusly:
This study calls for:

1. Careful reading from works listed in the syllabus–the introductory syllabus on technical services as well as later syllabi that will be distributed.
2. Close attention to class assignments, discussion, guests, etc.
3. Consultation with your assigned electronic "pen pal." Feel free to consult with other librarians that you may know. (The latter is not a requirement.) It is also permissible to consult with the instructor if you wish to do so.

   Professional librarians consult with one another in many ways–for example, with local colleagues; colleagues in networks of various kinds; through professional associations and conferences. The Internet has opened up new avenues for communication. Listservs allow for the sharing of ideas, concerns, questions, and information.

   In this class each of you will be matched up with electronic "pen pals" (maybe a better term would be "keyboard pals," but what's in a name?)–practicing librarians who day-by-day work in some area of technical services or are closely related to those who do and wrestle with the problems and issues we will be covering. Each librarian has agreed to participate in this project and to take time from his/her already busy schedule to work with you where appropriate. It is assumed that you will consult with them no more than two or three times during the pursuit of this project, will have well formulated questions or issues to discuss, and will not abuse the privilege. It is also assumed that you will acknowledge the source of their ideas that you incorporate into the paper just as you would cite information gathered from a publication. And as a courtesy, it is also assumed that it will be appropriate for you to write a thank you note to "your" librarians at the end of the study and copy me in on the acknowledgement.

   Names, affiliations, and addresses will be supplied to each of you individually.
4. A written assignment (no more than 10 pages) that explores and addresses the points listed below. (You may choose to make this a general paper or orient it toward a particular type of library.)

    a. The current state-of-the art of technical services in general as you see the picture. (Technical services is here defined as those functions relating to acquiring, organizing, and preserving materials. We won't be discussing cataloging *per se* so use your judgement about including it.)

    b. The question as to whether technical services will continue to be a viable service. (Justify or defend your answer.)

    c. How technology has affected technical services in the last two decades with your own thoughts about how it is likely to affect it in the future—e.g., organization, personnel, functions, training and continuing education. Do not neglect the consideration of the effect on libraries that do not have state-of-the-art technology.

    d. The role of the various players in the technical services arena—professional librarians, support staff, vendors, "outsourcers," professional associations, bibliographic utilities, networks, etc. The role of committee work in the life of technical services personnel.

    e. Discussion of questions and issues raised in the "Some Reflections" section discussed below.

    f. The future of technical services (unless you have already covered this in other sections).

5. SOME REFLECTIONS from the INSTRUCTOR and OTHERS to be CONSIDERED in the written study. You do not need to answer every single question in the Reflection Questions but you should cover most of the aspects in one way or another depending upon how you formulate your work.

Included in the "Reflections" category were statements and questions related to:

    a. Technology and technical services;

    b. Who are technical services librarians and what do they do? Where their programmatic duties and responsibilities originate;

    c. Rivalry between technical and public services librarians. Will the "virtual library" require more of the team approach?

    d. Outsourcing and its effects on technical services;

e. Librarians as preservers of information.

Specific readings in the "Reflections" section included:

- Hauptman, Robert and Carol L. Anderson. "The People Speak: the Dispersion and Impact of Technology in American Libraries" *Information Technology and Libraries* 13(4) (Dec. 1994): 249-256.
- Veaner, Allen. "Paradigm Lost, Paradigm Regained: a Persistent Personnel Issue in Academic Librarianship II" *College & Research Libraries* 55(5) (Sept. 1994): 389-402.
- Lewis, David W. "Making Academic Reference Services Work" *College & Research Libraries* 55(5) (Sept. 1994): 445-456.
- Drabenstott, Karen M. *Analytical Review of the Library of the Future.* Washington, Council on Library Resources, February 1994.
- Younger, Jennifer A. "Virtual Support: Evolving Technical Services" (In *The Virtual Library: Visions and Realities,* edited by Laverna M. Saunders. Westport, CT, Meckler, 1993, p. 71-86).
- *The Future is Now: the Changing Face of Technical Services.* Dublin, OH, OCLC Online Computer Library Center, 1994.
- Articles from *Library Acquisitions: Practice and Theory* 18(4) 1994 on outsourcing.

These readings were, of course, to be augmented by others listed in the more comprehensive course syllabus.

PROBLEMS

Although the instructions stated that the consultation of mentors was an integral part of the project and the majority of the students acted accordingly, there were a few "glitches" which can be corrected when this project is used again. Here were some of the main problems:

1. In a few cases, contact was not made early enough with the mentors. Although the necessity of early contact was stressed

from the beginning (three months before the deadline), it seems that some students (even at the graduate level) will put off even a major paper until "the last minute." Procrastination on the part of a few students resulted in pressure on the mentors and in some cases the inability of the mentors to respond. Careful planning is always a part of every librarian's life and the students learned this valuable lesson, too. The dedication of the mentors was amazing although not surprising. When a student did not contact a mentor, the mentor contacted the instructor indicating concern about the student and his/her well-being.

2. There were some problems concerning asking questions and making comments. A few students felt embarrassed to ask questions of experienced librarians or to engage in "conversation" with them. Some students felt they should try to solve problems on their own and not ask others. Others thought their questions might be considered naive by the mentors; this was a needless worry—the mentors often commented on the perceptive questions and comments of the students.

3. A few mentors were at the ACRL Conference in Pittsburgh about the time the paper was due and were not able to reply promptly. Again, better planning on the part of the students would have helped.

Most of the above problems can be dealt with in another offering. Some of the following procedures might lead to improvement:

1. Make more definite requirements about deadlines and follow up on students who do not meet these requirements. While an instructor does not enjoy admitting that graduate students require this kind of surveillance, apparently some few do need such reminders.

2. Provide students with some *required* questions to start conversations with the mentors. Some questions were hinted at but not required. Posing some sample questions might help the students who have difficulty getting started with a dialogue.

3. Require reporting on conversations with mentors throughout the semester rather than relying solely on the final paper.

Again, this would encourage working on the project through-out the semester and discourage "last minuteism."
4. Require that the instructor be copied in on the initial mes-sages. This step would allow the instructor to know that com-munication had begun.

EVALUATION BY STUDENTS

Aside from the previously mentioned problems most students had a positive feeling about the project. This assessment was made after reading the anonymous end-of-the-semester evaluations received several weeks after the course was completed and grades had been assigned; the "thank you" messages sent to mentors; the messages sent to the instructor; and the open discussion at the last class meeting. Several months later, some were still mentioning it and suggesting to the instructor that mentoring be continued.

Students felt that they had learned much from their mentors. Learning in class sessions was validated through these discussions. They were impressed with the involvement of mentors not only in their work but in committees and in professional associations. Actual contact in this manner broadened the students' knowledge base and provided new pragmatic as well as theoretical perspec-tives. One student noted that students were shown "models of pro-fessionalism whose actions and attitudes may have as great an impact as the content of their communications."

Often the students found the responses of the mentors much more to the point than were discussions of the issues in the literature. Especially appreciative were those interested in public librarianship since technical services in public libraries seems less well covered in the literature.

The students were impressed with the breadth and depth of the mentors' knowledge of the field in general. Apparently they had previously believed that the field had become so specialized that knowledge of other aspects than one's specialty was not a general requirement despite the fact that the instructor had told them other-wise. Most felt the experience had broadened their own perception of librarianship and the students were helped, in the words of one of them, to develop "insights into technical services work that have caused me to rethink many of my old assumptions about the present and future of libraries of all kinds."

In addition, the students learned about the commitment and dedication of library professionals. One student related that he had shown printouts of his mentors' responses to a friend from another field. The friend could not believe that professional librarians would spend so much time and effort to help a student. Wisely, the student took the opportunity to speak about the service aspects of librarianship (the "ethos of librarianship" as he characterized it).

EVALUATION BY MENTORS

To evaluate the project from the mentors' point of view, the instructor sent a series of eight questions (by e-mail, of course) to each mentor after the semester had ended. A synthesis of the questions and the replies follows.

1. *What was the amount of time you spent in participating?*

The range here was broad: from 1 hour to 20 hours. Some answers were vague: "not much really," "a couple of hours for each student," or "a few hours." Most responses were in the 4-8 hour range. Always encouraging is a remark such as this: "Actually, I would have been happy to put in more time." No respondent found the time factor to be burdensome even though many did this on "their own time."

2. *What type of preparation did you have to do to answer the questions or to comment?*

Many of the respondents indicated that the most time was spent thinking and organizing their thoughts preparatory to making responses to questions and comments. Many of them thought about their past and current personal experiences related to technical services. Some noted that they were already thinking about these issues or working on similar problems before participating in the project. A few consulted with other librarians in their own setting to get a handle on aspects of their library for which they were not directly responsible (e.g., catalog librarians talked to acquisitions or preservation librarians). Some gathered statistical or annual report information for the students, thereby acquiring additional information about their own libraries. One recent graduate looked over her own course notes and the syllabus used in the course several years earlier while another, who began her technical services career in 1973, reflected on the continuing changes since that time, noting that "the reflection showed that the last couple of years have been marked by escalating changes, particularly in communications (as demonstrated by this e-mail mentoring project)." Many of the mentors also read the articles assigned to the students and looked for related articles as they thought about the issues raised in the articles.

3. *How, if in any way, did this contribute to your own continuing education or make you think through what you are doing on the job?*

Almost universally the mentors responded that the experience made them *think* as well as organize and clarify their own thoughts on issues not only raised by the students but also "hot" issues they were currently facing in their own libraries, particularly outsourcing and digital libraries. The pressures of day-to-day activities leave little time for deep reflection and wide reading. The "luxury" of having time to read as was required in library school was a happy revisiting of an earlier day (when reading probably didn't seem such a happy circumstance!). While librarians suggested citations, some were appreciative of suggestions the students made to the practitioners. Some librarians found that through discussions with students they were once again focusing on larger issues rather than the "nitty-gritty" of solving the latest daily emergency. Likewise, some mentors were reminded of being part of a larger library community. "It reinforced [the fact] that library principles and standards that we adhere to (or should adhere to) are based on commonalities shared nationwide and internationally." The need for wider involvement in librarianship and in projects connecting beginning and experienced members of the profession was also acknowledged as a learning experience.

Perhaps this section was best summarized by one participant who considered this a useful continuing education experience "especially because it was an opportunity to read a set of carefully chosen articles related to the same general theme, to have a group of particular questions in mind while reading and thinking about them, and finally to respond to the articles and the questions in written form."

  4. *What were the kinds of questions the students asked or what did they want to know?*

While there were many different questions reported, most of them fell within several identifiable categories:

  a. *Technical services trends*

As might have been expected, this category seemed to be one about which almost all students had some questions to ask their mentors. The students were interested in the state of the art of technical services including the changes in organization that they had read about in class. The major responsibilities of technical services in academic and public libraries and the differences in technical services between the types of libraries were also favorite questions, as was whether the mentor saw the predicted-by-some demise of technical services to be a coming reality. Most students were also interested in how technology had affected the services and wanted to hear speculation concerning how the mentor expected technology to influence technical services further. Changes (other than technological) were also explored. As might be expected, the students were especially interested in having opinions of practicing librarians concerning the very current topic of outsourcing. The students also indicated they were aware of new trends but needed to understand more fully how they are implemented in reality.

Students were also interested in the mentors' thoughts concerning specialized technical services units versus holistic librarianship. The use of the Internet in technical services work was another favorite topic.

  b. *Role of professional vs. paraprofessional in technical services*

Many aspects of this relationship were explored by the students; for example, they were interested in how professional work is distinct from that of paraprofessionals and how the professional librarian identified which responsibilities to delegate to support staff.

c. *Relationship between public and technical services librarians*

Previously cited in this paper among the required readings for the "Think Piece" paper was an article by David W. Lewis. He suggested that technical services functions be streamlined and that increased use be made of outsourcing such functions. His contention was that potential savings could then be diverted to reference services. It was, therefore, not surprising that students would elicit comments concerning the relationship between technical and public services librarians as well as the allocation of funds to the two services.

d. *The mentor's position*

These were personal questions that asked about likes/dislikes in the individual mentor's position. Students were also interested in the backgrounds of their mentors and whether the mentors always wanted to work in the technical services area. Management aspects were also a popular area for questions.

e. *Status, etc., of technical services librarians*

The students were interested in whether there was a difference in perception among faculty and administration in academic libraries concerning public and technical services librarians. They were also concerned about participation in academic committees and in committee work in general. Publication and research requirements were investigated.

f. *Education-related questions*

The students wanted to know whether librarians believed that present-day schools were de-emphasizing technical services. They had more personal questions, too, such as: what technical services courses the mentors had enrolled in; what skills they believed should be learned in school and what ones were best learned on the job. Students asked for help in selecting recommended courses to become a technical services librarian or to become a specialist such as a serials cataloger.

g. *Miscellaneous*

As graduation was near at hand for some, job hunting strategies were sought. Also, as they approached the "real world," the students were interested in the overall direction of librarianship as seen by the mentors.

5. *Would you participate again in such an endeavor?*

A simple "yes" or "no" answer was anticipated but most respondents did not stop with a simple "yes." (There were no negative answers.) The "yes" answers were followed by statements such as "It was fun, interesting, stimulating," "I found mentoring to be very rewarding," "I would love to. I felt that the project gave me an entirely different way to have an impact on the profession, and a connection to its future than I would otherwise have had," "Definitely," "I certainly would."

6. *Is this a good use of electronic communications capabilities? Why?*

All of the answers here were also in the affirmative. They are telling because they indicate how quickly (in only a few years) those librarians fortunate enough to have this electronic capability have become dependent upon it. While this project could have been carried out without electronic capabilities it would have required much more time, effort, and resources on the part of everyone. But let's allow the mentors to tell us their viewpoints:

- "It gives mentors a chance to think about things they otherwise would not have thought about. It gives students a chance to meet and talk with people they would not otherwise have met. It gives us all a chance to learn to use this 'expanded neural network' to good effect and hopefully not be overloaded by what it can do for us."

- "For any student there is likely the feeling that what is being discussed in the classroom is mostly in a vacuum. Here is one way in which the student has an opportunity to make contact with someone who is functioning as a librarian. The dialogue possible through this medium allows for little intrusion upon the practicing librarian's time. Communication can take place at the convenience of the two parties. I suppose letters could achieve the same thing, but that means does have a more formal context to it."
- "It is speedy yet both parties can answer at a time convenient to the individual [with] not both parties having to be available at the same time."
- "E-mail is more informal . . . faster, but it gives one more time to think than phone communication . . . "
- "It uses e-mail to arrange unobtrusive communication between two persons who otherwise probably would not be in contact. This method is less invasive than a phone call, and quicker and less formal than a written letter."
- "No one had to make an appointment, be present in the prescribed place at an agreed upon time . . . The student had time to consider the questions and the respondent had time to consider the replies. It is a good blend of structure and spontaneity."
- "A good way to build collegiality."
- "This project is the sort of use of electronic communications which one hears about frequently (usually in rhapsodies, and in the abstract) but experiences more rarely. It's a quick and cost-effective way to connect the classroom with practitioners in a variety of circumstances and geographic locations."
- "Bridging the gap between the experienced librarian and graduate student contributes to the quality of library service in our communities. E-mail is an excellent conduit."
- "E-mail has great potential for reducing or removing barriers that have always existed such as distance . . . [and] procrastination . . . This specific use of e-mail is also excellent because it taps a wealth of expertise across the country for the students."

- "I am very difficult to catch by phone and it has sadly been months since I wrote a letter . . . I am in and out of my e-mail account many times each day and it is very easy to dash off a note, or even a long response, while I am there. There is also the advantage of starting a response, saving it, then going back and revising it before sending it."
- "A lot of times people in technical services have very little outside contact . . . Through e-mail one does not have to leave the building to have outside contact. I think it rekindles a person's interest in her job if someone else is also interested."
- "It allowed for conversation and thoughtful reflection. Much of what I use electronic resources for is of a passive nature, but this was interactive."

Several mentors were new to e-mailing and found it an opportunity to learn more about the medium. One did not have a user-friendly system and found the means difficult only because of this factor. Several persons regretted not being able to meet their students in person. In reality, eight students (one-third) did meet their e-mail mentors: two mentors were local; four students met their mentors when the mentors spoke to the class; the mentor for two of them came to visit on campus for reasons other than this class; and one student travelled to a library fifty miles away to visit her mentor.

7. *Did you feel as if you had a role in the education of a current student? Why?*

The respondents were quite modest in their responses to this question although the majority felt they had in some ways played the role of an active educator. The student papers indicated that indeed the mentors had played important educational roles. Most of the respondents did believe that they had something worthwhile to contribute. But several found the experiences to be "a two-way street": "I think you and they also educated me by making me think. . . . In explaining something, I clarified it in my mind." This sentiment was expressed by others such as the following: "It . . . gave me an opportunity to reflect on what has transpired in librarianship and academia over the past generation as the computer has penetrated ever more deeply into things and finally [it] gave me a chance to try to generalize from some of these experiences. I think this is being professional on a level which has been quite difficult in the past because of the slowness of mail, the expense of the phone and other limitations imposed by distance." Others, too, felt that sharing expertise was indeed part of being a professional—"why reinvent the wheel when there is so much wisdom to share with one another?" Certainly those of us who are teachers should ask ourselves that question more often.

8. *Did this experience make you feel "closer" to GSLIS? Why?*

An unexpected result of this project began to evolve as positive unsolicited reactions came from the mentors concerning their being asked to be a part of this project at GSLIS. As noted earlier, all but one mentor held a degree from GSLIS. Increasingly, academic institutions find it important to keep in touch with their graduates if only for fund-raising initiatives. This project had no "ulterior" motives and this question was included in the final evaluation because of initial responses from the mentors.

- "It was an ego boost for the older [generation]."
- "It was very nostalgic to receive a multi-page colored handout full of provocative questions and useful references [and] to work through it in something of the way . . . I did when I was there. The communication with a current student also made me feel in touch with the school."
- "Yes, very much. It's nice to know you're not completely forgotten once you leave GSLIS! While all of us wish we could afford to make substantial monetary contributions to GSLIS fund-raisers, sadly, the realities of academic pay generally preclude that possibility. But I feel I have contributed something worthwhile to my alma mater in helping out with a class."
- "Yes, and quite nostalgic!"
- "A positive connection! I had an opportunity to think about and try to articulate the intellectual interest—excitement, even—of applying and seeing the implications of principles I had learned many years ago in library school, in our changing circumstances. I had a chance to step back from my activities and consider the ways they fit together. And the students,

themselves, with their interesting questions and responses, were mentors for me, too. They generously gave me the opportunity to practice being a colleague to a new generation of librarians."

- "[As a] part-time former [student], I never developed a real sense of belonging there. By having contact with students who were going through a class I had also taken, who were having thoughts similar to those I had at that point in my program, and discussing issues I am currently involved in, I felt much closer to the process than I ever did while in school."

- "Yes . . . I have not had a chance to return since I received my degree [a quarter of century ago], but I often recall my experiences there."

One respondent offered yet a further outreach for mentoring. Her suggestion was to assign a mentor in the same way each new student is assigned a faculty advisor. She felt this would be "an excellent opportunity for fledgling librarians to begin those all-so-important networking connections. . . . It is also a good way for the alumni to participate in the propagation of the profession, and to keep up with what's going on in the classroom. I can see some real possibilities here. Sign me up!"

Appreciation of learning the content and methods of present day classes was a consistent theme of the responses to this question.

CONCLUSION

No project, no assignment, is ever perfect and this one had its share of problems, some of which have already been detailed. One of the first lessons learned here was that for some persons human communication is always difficult. Ways must be found to ease those entering the profession into taking that first step of communicating with those already working in the profession. What had not been anticipated as a difficulty really proved to be a stumbling block for a few students. Teaching people to take the first step, while difficult for some, may lead to positive interactions in the future. We live in a new age of electronic communications–we owe it to our students to prepare them to participate in this environment.

These students learned something about doing that while the mentors, too, learned of new potentials as did the instructor. While other means of communication might have had similar results, just as was demonstrated by the use of regular mail, the phone and an on-site visit in one special instance, the alternative process would be more difficult, costly, and time consuming. Geographic locations and distances are no longer factors. One student noted "the pedagogical potential [for a project like this] is promising." The instructor agrees. The "facelessness" of e-mail did not appear to be a real problem—in fact, it may have helped some of those students who were more reluctant to seek advice. Exchange of photographs might be one method of "giving a face" to participants.

Devising the project, contacting mentors, developing strategies, reassuring both mentors and those being mentored and following up with both groups demanded a great deal more instructor time than a typical required paper would have called for; however, as indicated by responses from both groups, the efforts had positive results for all, including the instructor. When others ask to use one's ideas or volunteer to become participants, one is encouraged that there has been some success. Similar mentoring ideas are being discussed in other contexts at GSLIS. Two instructors in two different schools have asked to adopt or adapt the idea for their courses. Especially encouraging is the fact that the mentors want to do it again; some students asked to be placed on the mentor list when they are in the "real world" (in fact, one student from the spring 1995 class has already received permission from her supervisor to be a mentor). Librarians who have heard about the project but were not a part of the original group have volunteered their services. Whether it was the *means* of communication or just the opportunity to communicate that was more important, one cannot tell. Perhaps it was both.

Jennifer Cargill expressed the opinion that "mentorships benefit the profession, libraries, and individuals. They hasten career development, promote networking, and link generations of leaders."[2] In retrospect, this project was an attempt to accomplish those goals. The author expresses her gratitude to the following persons for their enthusiastic response to this networking, linking, and learning experience.

Students in LIS 437, spring 1995, were:
Hui-lan Hsu (Abby) Chen, Barbara Shelton Childers, Ximena Chrisagis, Donshan Gao, Scott F. Gillies, Anne E. Hull, Heather A. Jagman, Ann E. Kempke, Shun-wa Lee, Carol Lepzelter, Jing Liao, Russell L. Martin, Michelle A. Mayes, Sarah H. McDougal, John S. McInnis, Wai-chi Mok, Clarice Mushlin, Eric R. Norton, Elaine Fetyko Page, Robert C. Richards, Jr., Marina S. Savoie, Hong Yu, AnnMarie Ziadie.

Mentors were:
David G. Anderson, Head Catalog Department, William Russell Pullen Library, Georgia State University, Atlanta, GA

Melvin Carlson, Jr., Assistant Head and Senior Cataloger, University of Massachusetts, Amherst, MA

Ruth C. Carter, Assistant Director for Automated and Technical Services, Hillman Library, University of Pittsburgh, Pittsburgh, PA

Hui-Yee Chang, Serials Cataloger/Senior Assistant Librarian, Coe Library, University of Wyoming, Laramie, WY

Linda C. Ewbank, General Original Cataloger, Hillman Library, University of Pittsburgh, Pittsburgh, PA

Steve Hardin, Senior Assistant Librarian, Cunningham Memorial Library, Indiana State University, Terre Haute, IN

Steven D. Harsin, Head, Acquisitions Department, Loyola University Chicago, Chicago, IL

Marianne Hebert, Head of Technical Services, Purchase College, SUNY, Purchase, NY

William T. Henderson, Preservation Librarian, University of Illinois at Urbana-Champaign, Urbana, IL

Sue Jiang, Systems Librarian, Washington University, St. Louis, MO

Kuang-Hwei (Janet) Lee-Smeltzer, Catalog Librarian, Kerr Library, Oregon State University, Corvallis, OR

Y. Mei Mah, Catalog and Systems Librarian, Warren Wilson College, Asheville, NC

Larry Millsap, Head Bibliographic Records, University of California, Santa Cruz, Santa Cruz, CA

Debbie Morrow, Automation Librarian, University Library, Grand Valley State University, Allendale, MI

Carolynne Myall, Head of Collection Services, University Libraries, Eastern Washington University, Cheney, WA

Steven J. Oberg, Head, Bibliographic Control (formerly Serials Cataloger), University of Chicago Library, Chicago, IL

Lori L. Osmus, Head, Serials and Monographs Original Cataloging Department, Iowa State University, Ames, IA

Rick Ralston, Automated Processing Manager, Ruth Lilly Medical Library, Indiana University, Indianapolis, IN

Frances E. Roehm, Adult Services Reference Librarian, Bloomington Public Library, Bloomington, IL

Karen Schneider, Doctoral Student, School of Information and Library Studies, University of Michigan, Ann Arbor, MI (formerly, Consultant, Wayne, NJ)

Elizabeth M. Schobernd, Preservation Librarian, Milner Library, Illinois State University, Normal, IL

Anita Schuneman, Chief Cataloger, University of Colorado at Denver, Denver, CO

Meredith L. Smith, Assistant Acquisitions Librarian and Visiting Research Associate, Library, University of Illinois at Urbana-Champaign, Urbana, IL

Esther Turoci, Manager, Technical Services, Westerville Public Library, Westerville, OH

Eloise M. Vondruska, Head, Catalog Department, School of Law Library, Northwestern University, Chicago, IL

Yuan Zhou, Head, East Asian Library, University of Minnesota Libraries, Minneapolis, MN

REFERENCES AND NOTES

1. After the project was underway, the writer saw a listserv message from Anne Woodsworth (Dean, Palmer School of Library and Information Science, Long Island University) that explained a course mentoring project that she had used. The choice of mentors and the way in which mentors worked with her class were different from the project at GSLIS. After LIS 437 was completed in May 1995, the instructor read an article in the July 1995 (56(4): 352-361) issue of *College & Research Libraries* by Tami Echavarria, W. Bede Mitchell, Karen Liston Newsome, Thomas A. Peters, and Deleyne Wentz entitled "Encouraging

Research through Electronic Mentoring: a Case Study" which described an experiment using electronic mail to create mentoring relationships that focused on research in library and information science. Again, this was a much different type of project than the one described in this article.

2. Jennifer Cargill. "Developing Library Leaders: the Role of Mentorship" *Library Administration & Management* 3 (winter 1989): 14.

The BUBL Information Service

Joanne Gold

SUMMARY. The BUBL Information Service is arguably one of the most useful UK-based resources on the Internet for librarians and academics alike. Originating as part of a short-term networking project, the Service has overcome numerous obstacles in its development to a standard whereby it has been recognised, and funded, as a national information service by the Joint Information Systems Committee of the Higher Education Funding Councils of England, Scotland, Wales and the Department of Education for Northern Ireland. This article shall look at various aspects in the development of BUBL, highlight particular areas of the Service, and end by focusing on the direction the Service is moving in now. *[Article copies available for a fee from The Haworth Document Delivery Service: 1-800-342-9678. E-mail address: getinfo@haworth.com]*

TOWARDS A SECURE FUTURE

The BUBL Information Service originated in 1990, when an experimental BUlletin Board for Libraries (BUBL) was created as part of Project Jupiter–an initiative based at Glasgow University which aimed to train librarians in the use of JANET. Funding for Project Jupiter ended in May 1991, leaving the future of the newly

Joanne Gold is Information Officer with the BUBL Information Service, Andersonian Library, 101 St. James' Road, Glasgow, G4 0NS, Scotland (E-mail: j.gold@strath.ac.uk).

[Haworth co-indexing entry note]: "The BUBL Information Service." Gold, Joanne. Co-published simultaneously in *The Serials Librarian* (The Haworth Press, Inc.) Vol. 29, No. 3/4, 1996, pp. 165-174; and: *Serials Management in the Electronic Era: Papers in Honor of Peter Gellatly, Founding Editor of* The Serials Librarian (ed: Jim Cole, and James W. Williams) The Haworth Press, Inc., 1996, pp. 165-174. Single or multiple copies of this article are available for a fee from The Haworth Document Delivery Service [1-800-342-9678, 9:00 a.m. - 5:00 p.m. (EST). E-mail address: getinfo@haworth.com].

established BUBL somewhat in the balance. Fortunately the service was saved from extinction by a group of librarians from the University of Strathclyde who realised the potential benefit which BUBL had for the UK's developing library and information science networking community. Over the next few years it was their voluntary efforts which maintained BUBL. During the same period the Service grew in popularity, with BUBL even attracting small amounts of sponsorship money from commercial and professional organisations. These were obviously welcomed, but were not enough to maintain the expanding BUBL in the long term.

The first significant breakthrough in terms of the long-term survival of the Service came in January 1994, when the Joint Information Systems Committee (JISC) agreed to fund the maintenance and development of BUBL for one year. The relative security which this brought allowed BUBL to enter a new phase in its development. For the first time the Service was able to plan for more than just the immediate future, and could employ a full-time member of staff to take on the newly created post of BUBL Information Officer. A further year's funding was received from the JISC to cover 1995, and while this made the position of BUBL secure for another twelve months, the long-term survival of BUBL was still not inevitable. With the doubt always remaining of what would happen to BUBL when the one-year funding came to an end, planning for the future was not without difficulties. It was therefore welcome news when, in January 1995, the JISC confirmed that BUBL was to be funded as a UK national information service, to provide a subject-based service encompassing all subject areas, alongside its specialist Library and Information Science service. This put funding on a three yearly cycle, and the future of the Service on a much firmer footing.

BUBL BATH

When the experimental BUlletin Board for Libraries was set up, it was based at Glasgow University, and run on USERBUL software. By 1991, however, a move to new software was necessitated. In part this was due to the fact that the USERBUL software was no longer being developed, but perhaps had more to do with the growing importance, and use, of the Internet in the UK. Coinciding as this did with the impending demise of the Vax at Glasgow University, it was arranged that the Service be re-located to Bath University, and to the UKOLN server there. Subsequently, instead of being run over a JANET link between the Universities of Strathclyde and Glasgow, from September 1993 BUBL was run over a JANET link between the Universities of Strathclyde and Bath. This re-location of BUBL to Bath inevitably brought with it the odd joke, but more importantly it meant a move for BUBL on to Gopher and World Wide Web server software with multimedia facilities (see Figure 1).

Although the location of the BUBL server had changed, management and maintenance of the Service did not, and remained the responsibility of the voluntary staff (and, from January 1994, the BUBL Information Officer) based at Strathclyde University Library.

BRANCHING OUT FROM LIBRARY AND INFORMATION SCIENCE

The move to Bath, and onto Gopher and WWW software, enabled BUBL to become established on the Internet, and provide organised access to the wide range of resources and services available over the network. Greatly expanded coverage for the Service resulted, and

FIGURE 1. The BUBL Information Service—home page.

 The BUBL Information Service

- ☐ The Subject Tree - all subjects including Library and Information Science
- ☐ About BUBL, BUBL services, convergence with LINK

|Home||Subject Tree||New||Features| |Site-reps||Other Services||Internet search||WWW|

JISC, Tell Us, Copyright

furthered the move away from a remit which was specific to LIS, towards one which included a specialist LIS service as part of a far broader, and largely subject-based, approach.

When BUBL was first established, the specific aim of the Service had been to function as a bulletin board on JANET for the academic library community. However, it soon became apparent that much of the information being made available on BUBL was not only of direct interest to, but was actually being used by, the wider academic and research community; non-librarians. This was confirmed as being the case when, in March 1994, a survey was carried out in order to assess who was using BUBL, and for what purposes. A very short questionnaire was sent out to the LIS networking community over LIS-LINK, the Mailbase (mainly UK-based) library-oriented discussion list. Of the 245 responses, 20% indicated that they were non-librarians using BUBL directly for wider Internet access. Since these were replies to a survey sent over a list intended specifically for librarians it was inferred that the actual percentage of non-librarians using BUBL would make up significantly more than 20% of BUBL's total users. This movement away from actually being, and from being perceived as, a service aimed at and used by librarians was reflected at the same time by a change in name, from The BUlletin Board for Libraries to The BUBL Information Service.

THE BUBL SUBJECT TREE

The subject-based approach mentioned above was realised through the BUBL Subject Tree, an initiative which began in the final quarter of 1993 (just after the move to Bath). BUBL was the first national UK service to offer its users subject-based access to the Internet and, while others have followed the example set, it remains the only UK national service whose subject tree covers all main subject areas. By arranging resources according to their subject area, and according to UDC (with an alphabetical alternative now also available), BUBL was among the first to provide its users with library-professional-enhanced, and user-friendly access to the Internet (see Figure 2).

For the most part the subject tree was created, and is maintained, by BUBL staff. However, BUBL also has a group of "subject specialists," mostly librarians, who contribute to the maintenance and development of the subject tree. Working on a voluntary basis, the subject specialists take responsibility for particular areas of the tree, these relating to their own specialisms. The subject specialists recommend to BUBL resources to be added to their particular subject area, with advice on how these should be organised.

Links recommended by subject specialists, along with those located by BUBL staff, are added to the subject tree on a daily basis, and at the end of each week a list of links added to the subject tree during the week is compiled and sent as an Internet resources current awareness bulletin to LIS-LINK. This list is also made available on the BUBL web server in hypertext format, allowing users to link directly from any given addition to the resource itself.

The main aim of the Subject Tree initiative was to provide users of BUBL with improved and organised access to the wide range of electronic resources and services made freely available over the Internet, and this has undoubtedly been achieved. By branching out from library and information science the subject tree has allowed BUBL's user base to grow, and has developed into perhaps the most significant of the services offered by the BUBL Information Service. See <URL: http://www.bubl.bath.ac.uk/BUBL/cattree.html>. A tree approach was never regarded as adequate, however, and dissatisfaction with this eventually led to the CATRIONA project, and subsequently, to the new LINK service (see below).

NETWORKING PROJECTS

When first established, BUBL aimed to encourage, develop, co-ordinate and support the emerging LIS networking community in the UK, and to promote its interests. As this community has emerged so BUBL has been involved in supporting and co-ordinating its development, and through various means has been active in informing, and providing facilities to, UK librarians and other information specialists engaged in the provision of Internet-resource-based services to the UK academic and research community.

A number of projects have been used by BUBL as part of this LIS community networking development process. In the first instance, when BUBL was running a gopher server alone members

FIGURE 2. BUBL WWW Mathematics Resources: an example of a subject-specialist maintained area of the BUBL Subject Tree. Maintained by Ian Winship, University of Northumbria at Newcastle.

 The BUBL Information Service

BUBL WWW Subject Tree

| Subject Tree: UDC or Alphabetical| |BUBL Home Page|

BUBL WWW Mathematics Resources

Contents:

> Bibliographies
> Discussion Lists
> Education and Teaching
> Electronic Journals
> General Services
> Numerical Routines
> Preprints
> Software

Bibliographies

Numerical Methods
> Index to International journal for numerical methods in engineering and Comunications in numerical methods in engineering
MathSearch
> Search Engine for searching over 19.000 maths and statistics documents across the Internet

|Return to Contents at top of page|

Discussion Lists

Kovacs - Mathematics, Statistics
> From the Directory of Scholarly Electronic Conferences (9th Revision)

|Return to Contents at top of page|

Education and Teaching

Calculus and Mathematica
> Project using Mathematica to teach calculus to high school and college students
Cornell
> Cornell Mathematics Gateway - resources for grades 9-12
CTI
> CTI Centre for Mathematics and Statistics
CWI Research Institute
> Research in Mathematics and Computer Science
Geometry Forum
> Software. discussion list archives and other educational resources
Hub
> Hub Mathematics Center
IMSC
> Institute of Mathematical Science - research institute (India)
Magic
> MathMagic
Math and Science Education

of the LIS community were encouraged to become BUBL "section editors" by contributing to particular areas of the gopher server, and taking responsibility for their maintenance. This was made possible by facilities which allowed section editors to mail items direct to the server, and a number of users did become, and continue to be, involved in this voluntary effort. Perhaps because they saw the benefits it had for libraries and librarians, one area of the gopher server in particular has attracted section editor volunteers. This is Section E2–BUBL's Tables of Contents and Abstracts Service, which provides tables of contents and abstracts (where available) of around 300 journals, the majority of which are LIS-oriented. See <URL:gopher://ukoln.bath.ac.uk:7070/11/BUBL_Main_Menu/E>. The Subject Tree initiative (details of which were outlined above) has also encouraged voluntary effort, with users taking responsibility for the development of certain areas of the Tree. In both of these initiatives members of the LIS community have used the networks not only to cooperate with BUBL and be involved in a successful networking project, but to do so to the benefit of other members of their community by providing resources of use and interest for their perusal in a centralised location.

A number of other co-operative networking projects have been initiated by BUBL, these including LIS-SYS and LIS-SITEREPS. The LIS-SYS project was set up in late 1994 to organise a worksharing initiative in which systems librarians, and other IT specialists, would co-operate to share the work involved in keeping up-to-date with IT applications in libraries. In doing so, the intention is that an area covering library systems and software will be built up on BUBL, and indeed this has begun, and can be viewed at <URL:http://www.bubl.bath.ac.uk/BUBL/LISSYS.html>. A Mailbase list of the same name has been set up as the method of communication for all involved in the project. The LIS-SITEREPS project began early in 1995, and aims to build stronger links between BUBL and its user community. This is being undertaken in conjunction with JUGL, the JANET User Group for Libraries, through the appointment of representatives at each JANET library site to act as a point of contact and liaison between that site and both BUBL and JUGL. A closer relationship with users and individual institutions is envisaged as developing out of this initiative, with representatives in a position to influence BUBL's course of development. A Mailbase list, also called lis-sitereps, has been established as the mechanism through which this will take place.

Projects, such as those mentioned here, have undoubtedly contributed towards developing a confident and active LIS networking community. A role for that community in the provision of network-based information services has also been established. Although BUBL now seeks increasingly to serve the wider community, and will continue to widen its scope and direction in the future, it will nevertheless continue to develop and promote LIS co-operation through such initiatives.

THE FUTURE

At the time of writing, a new service is under development at BUBL. It is planned that the service will be called LINK, this standing for Libraries of Networked Knowledge (see Figure 3). See <URL:http:// 130.159.84.5/>.

Building on the strong base BUBL now has as a JISC-funded national information service it is intended that LINK will improve on the quality and depth of service currently provided to BUBL users. In doing so it will be closely linked with a project which has developed as an offshoot of the BUBL Subject Tree initiative;

FIGURE 3. BUBL's LINK Service—home page.

☐ The Subject Libraries Internet resource libraries covering **all major subject areas**
☐ About LINK, Help: The Catalogue, Current Awareness Services, WWW, Z39.50, Gopher, Telnet, X.25 access, Contacts, Contributions, Tools, JISC, other sponsors

[Help] [Search] [New] [BUBL] [Tell us] [JISC] [Services by Type] [Tools] [Copyright] [Strathclyde]

CATRIONA-CATaloguing and Retrieval of Information Over Networks Applications. CATRIONA envisages a Z39.50-based distributed catalogue of Internet resources with libraries and library services playing a significant role in this.

Integral to the development of the new LINK service is a software donation recently made to BUBL, which has allowed the creation of a catalogued database, searchable in the style of a library OPAC, with searches possible by author, subject, title, UDC class number and by Boolean combination. The software has also enabled Z39.50 access to the service, offering the potential of BUBL access through library OPAC interfaces and (with Z39.50 OPAC clients like GEO-PAC and WINPAC) the possibility of electronic delivery to the desktop via the OPAC as envisaged in CATRIONA. Enhanced maintenance facilities are another feature, with automated URL checking, and GUI control of service menus, files and pages. These features will benefit both users and staff working on the service. The new service, LINK, will build upon and enhance the subject-based approach first established via the BUBL Subject Tree. The intention is that all resources on the service, or accessible via it, will be organised by subject, in Subject Libraries, and that these Subject Libraries will encompass all main subject areas. All resources contained within the Subject Libraries will be catalogued and will thus be accessible through the search facility available on every page of the service, as well as through Z39.50. The specialist Library and Information Science element which has been provided by BUBL from the beginning, will be continued through LINK, but it will be one of the many LIbraries of Networked Knowledge.

For more information on BUBL, contact Joanne Gold: j.gold@ strath.ac.uk
To subscribe to LIS-link, and receive the BUBL updates messages, send an e-mail to:
  mailbase@mailbase.ac.uk
  with the message:
  JOIN LIS-link Yourfirstname Yourlastname
  (e.g., JOIN LIS-link Joanne Gold)

GLOSSARY

BUBL–BUlletin Board for Libraries/BUBL Information Service
CATRIONA–CATaloguing and Retrieval of Information Over Networks Applications
GUI–Graphic User Interface
JANET–Joint Academic NETwork
JISC–Joint Information Systems Committee
JUGL–JANET User Group for Libraries
LINK–LIbraries of Networked Knowledge
UDC–Universal Decimal Classification
UKOLN–United Kingdom Office for Library and Information Networking
WWW–World Wide Web

REFERENCES

Nicholson, D., "BUBL and the development of the UK LIS networking community," *Vine 93*, December 1993:12-17

Nicholson, D., "BUBL, The Bulletin Board for Libraries," *Library and Information Briefings*, Double Issues 37/38, December 1992:22

Nicholson, D. et al., "Cataloguing the Internet: CATRIONA feasibility study," *Library and Information Research Report 105*, London: British Library Research & Development Department 1995

Wood, J., "BUBL and the Internet," *Assignation*, Vol. 12, No. 02, January 1995:21-25

Serial Sources on the Web

Jeanne M. K. Boydston

SUMMARY. The last few years have seen an unprecedented growth of the electronic environment in all areas of librarianship. Recently, the Internet and World Wide Web have been the focus of much of this expansion. Many specialized resources of interest to serials librarians can be found on the Web. This article briefly examines the World Wide Web, and a selected number of resources of interest primarily to serialists. *[Article copies available for a fee from The Haworth Document Delivery Service: 1-800-342-9678. E-mail address: getinfo@ haworth.com]*

INTRODUCTION

In recent years there has been unprecedented growth of the electronic environment in all areas of librarianship. Internet resources such as electronic mail, file transfer protocol (FTP), gopher, and most recently, the World Wide Web have fundamentally changed the ways in which librarians communicate information among themselves and to library patrons. Many specialized electronic resources exist for the technical services librarian. Among these, many are specifically geared to the needs and interests of serialists. This paper will focus on one area of electronic communication: World Wide Web home pages as they relate to serials librarianship.

Jeanne M. K. Boydston is Associate Professor and Serials Cataloger at Iowa State University Library, Ames, IA 50011-2140.

[Haworth co-indexing entry note]: "Serial Sources on the Web." Boydston, Jeanne M. K. Co-published simultaneously in *The Serials Librarian* (The Haworth Press, Inc.) Vol. 29, No. 3/4, 1996, pp. 175-187; and: *Serials Management in the Electronic Era: Papers in Honor of Peter Gellatly, Founding Editor of* The Serials Librarian (ed: Jim Cole, and James W. Williams) The Haworth Press, Inc., 1996, pp. 175-187. Single or multiple copies of this article are available for a fee from The Haworth Document Delivery Service [1-800-342-9678, 9:00 a.m. - 5:00 p.m. (EST). E-mail address: getinfo@haworth.com].

WORLD WIDE WEB HOME PAGES ON THE INTERNET

The Internet can be described as a network of networks which use the TCP/IP protocol to communicate with one another.[1] The World Wide Web, which is only one part of the Internet, is an information management system for the various documents contained in each network. Documents are coded with hypertext language allowing them to be seamlessly linked to one another. The user can easily access these documents and move from one to another. This link is achieved through a Universal Resource Locator (URL) which functions as a unique identifier for each home page similar to a mail address. The advantages of this link to the user are many. There isn't a need to learn a group of cumbersome and confusing commands and the response is, in most cases, almost instantaneous. The resulting document can be read online, printed or downloaded to a local system. Furthermore, the Web gives the user easy access to geographically remote databases. For example, using the Web, and a few keystrokes and mouse clicks, a librarian in Iowa can search the online catalog of a sister institution within the state or can access the online catalog of the Bodleian Library in Oxford, England.

WORLD WIDE WEB RESOURCES

Since its inception at the European Laboratory for Particle Physics (CERN) in the early 1990s, the Web has grown dramatically.[2] A December 1995 Web Crawler search on the query "serials librarianship" resulted in the retrieval of 19 documents. The words "serials cataloging" yielded 63 documents and "serials acquisitions" had 134 hits. The search engine Yahoo has also recently added a subdirectory for libraries that includes links to home pages for libraries worldwide, library related businesses, organizations and resources. In short, like much on the Web, librarianship is an area that is growing. This constantly changing picture can be rewarding and exciting, but also can lead to frustration. URLs may change without warning. There may or may not be online references providing a link from the old URL to the new, similar to an authority record's "see" reference. Information contained within home pages also may change without warning. Of course, any resource may change its information, but in a paper environment, the older edition still exists. In the electronic environment, unless the information has been saved somehow, it is often lost. On a positive note, the Web site can be updated easily and thus potentially have the most current information.

The size of the Web leads to the discovery of far more serials-related resources than could possibly be included in this article. Therefore, only a few representative resources are included. Many of the sites also contain an impressive array of hypertext links; therefore only a handful of representative links are included in the citations below. The information contained in the citations and revision dates is accurate as of April 1996. While this paper focuses on Web home pages, there are many other important serials-related electronic resources available. Two very useful sites are LC Marvel and the NASIG Gopher. A NASIG Web site is planned to be available in spring 1996.[3]

GENERAL

1. Libweb: Library Servers via WWW.
URL: http://sunsite.berkeley.edu/Libweb/
Scope: International.
Purpose: To provide access to Web home pages for libraries, library schools and library-related businesses.
Date last revised: April 10, 1996.
Representative links: Provides links to home pages of libraries (public and academic), library schools, library-related businesses, organizations, bibliographic utilities and Web access to Library catalog gateways.

2. SERIALST Scope & Purpose.
URL: http://www.uvm.edu/~bmaclenn/serialst.html#database
Scope: Information regarding the listserv SERIALST.
Date last revised: March 1996.
Representative links: Links to various electronic methods to retrieve SERIALST archives including gopher and Web sites.

Comments: This is the Web version of the Scope & Purpose statement for the newsgroup SERIALST.

ACQUISITIONS RESOURCES

3. ACQNET.
URL: http://www.library.vanderbilt.edu/law/acqs/acqnet.html
Scope: Contains information about the electronic journal ACQNET, welcoming document and archives. The archives are accessible via the Web home page, gopher and FTP; they are also searchable.
Date last revised: February 28, 1996.

4. AcqWeb.
URL: http://www.library.vanderbilt.edu/law/acqs/acqs.html
Scope: Monographic and serials acquisitions, international in scope.
Date last revised: March 8, 1996.
Representative links: Contains numerous links to publishers, associations, acquisitions home pages, conservation, bookbinding, electronic journals, newsletters, listserv archives and links to online library catalogs for verification purposes; also contains the meeting schedule for ALA Midwinter 1996.

5. Feather River Institute on Acquisitions, 1995.
URL: http://staffweb.lib.washington.edu/acq/feather.html
Scope: Summaries of the papers presented at the 1995 Institute, plus information on the 1996 Institute.
History: Only the current year's proceedings are listed.
Representative links: Entries include the presenters' email addresses, so they may be contacted for further information. Information is also included on next year's Institute. This is an unauthorized summary of the Institute contained on the University of Washington Library Home Page.

6. Newsletter on Serials Pricing Issues.
URL: http://sunsite.unc.edu/reference/prices/prices.html
Scope: Web access to the archives and current issues of the elec-

tronic journal *Newsletter on Serials Pricing Issues*; also contains information on the Newsletter including subscription directions.
Date last revised: August 9, 1995.

7. United States Book Exchange: Back Issues Shelf List.
URL: http://www.usbe.com/
Scope: Presents a shelf list of titles regularly stocked and available to member libraries.
Comments: The shelf list can be searched online; items can be ordered online by member libraries.

SERIALS CATALOGING RESOURCES

8. Internet Cataloging Project.
URL: http://www.oclc.org/oclc/man/catproj/catcall.htm
Scope: Contains both serial and monographic cataloging records for Internet-accessible materials.
Date last revised: Catalog updated April 3, 1996.
Comments: This is the home page for OCLC's Internet Cataloging Project. This project is an international effort to create and evaluate a searchable database for Internet-accessible materials. The searchable database provides access to both serial and monographic records, which can be displayed in either a labeled or MARC format. This is a valuable resource for libraries that are just starting to catalog this type of material. There is also information on the Project and on cataloging Internet resources, in general.

9. Internet Resources for Cataloging.
URL: http://asa.ugl.lib.umich.edu/chdocs/libcat/libcat.htm
Scope: Covers all aspects of cataloging and librarianship.
Date last revised: September 15, 1995.
Representative links: Vianne T. Sha has assembled a very extensive document with literally hundreds of links. Sha also gives information on how to access this document via the Web, gopher, telnet and FTP. Included are links to national libraries, professional associations, national bibliographic utilities, local library systems, cataloging tools and training resources, cataloging-related

software, references and an outline of the USMARC format 856 field.

10. Machine Readable Cataloging (MARC).
URL: http://lcweb.loc.gov/marc/
Scope: Information related to the MARC format.
Representative links: Information about format integration, MARBI minutes, MARC Advisory Committee proposals and discussion papers, MARC documentation. Many of the documents are searchable by keyword.

11. Serials in Cyberspace: Collections, Resources, and Services.
URL: http://www.uvm.edu:80/~bmaclenn/
Scope: Serials in general, with a special emphasis on sites with electronic journal collections.
Date last revised: April 8, 1996.
Representative links: As well as links to electronic journal topics, Birdie MacLennan has also included links to other useful sources such as IFLANET, the ISSN International Centre, Publishers' Catalogs Home Page, Tools for Serials Catalogers and LC Marvel, to name a few.

12. Tools for Serials Catalogers: A Collection of Useful Sites and Sources.
URL: http://www.library.vanderbilt.edu/ercelawn/serials.html
Scope: The focus here is on serials cataloging, but there are also some links that may be of interest to acquisitions.
Date last revised: April 1996.
Representative links: Ann Ercelawn has included links to sources for cataloging documentation (CONSER, LC Marvel, and OCLC), format integration, foreign language dictionaries, links to other technical services Web pages, professional development opportunities, discussion list archives, and ALCTS Committee to Study Serials Cataloging minutes for both Midwinter and Summer 1995.
Comments: One of the most comprehensive sources found in this study.

CONSERVATION

13. Conservation Online: Resources for Conservation Professionals (CoOL).
URL: http://palimpsest.stanford.edu/
Scope: Conservation of library, archives and museum materials.
Date last revised: April 10, 1996.
Representative links: Selected conservation topics, mailing list archives, and other resources on conservation.
Comments: While this page doesn't specifically address serials, many of the topics and links will have information that can be applied to serials, such as disaster planning and response, mass deacidification reports and statements of ethics.

PUBLISHERS AND VENDORS

This is only a small sample of the many home pages that are available from publishers and vendors. A fairly extensive list of links to publishers catalogs can be accessed through the Publishers' Catalogs Home Page (see citation below).

14. EBSCO Information Services.
URL: http://www.ebsco.com/
Purpose: To provide information about EBSCO's services and products.
Date last revised: April 4, 1995.

15. Faxon Company Home Page.
URL: http://www.faxon.com/
Purpose: To provide information about Faxon's services and products.
Date last revised: April 16, 1996.
Representative links: Provides some links to publishers on the Internet, various standards organizations, general documents about the Internet, conference information with some links to home pages for the host cities.

16. Readmore.

URL: http://www.readmore.com/

Scope: Readmore's publisher services, electronic service and Readmore's Information Library.

Date last revised: September 15, 1995.

Representative links: Information Library includes: links to electronic journals and newsletters, library catalogs, library-related organizations and companies, national libraries' Internet servers, international and national professional organizations, standards and standards organizations, general and notable collections, also ALA conference information at the appropriate times of the year. Also includes Backserv, an informal medium for the informal exchange of serial back issues and monographs.

17. Publishers' Catalogs Home Page.

URL: http://www.lights.com/publisher/

Scope: International.

Purpose: To provide links to publishers' catalogs home pages.

Representative links: International; database can be accessed by country and contains hundreds of links to publishers' home pages worldwide.

LIBRARIES

18. Bodleian Library (University of Oxford).

URL: http://www.bodley.ox.ac.uk/

Scope: International.

Representative links: Links to Bodleian's own OPAC and user guides, BARD (Bodleian Access to Remote Databases) which includes World Wide Web, gophers, Usenet, WAIS (Wide Area Information Services) and FTP. Even contains a link to the Bodleian Shopping Arcade.

19. BUBL Information Service Web Server.

URL: http://www.bubl.bath.ac.uk/BUBL/home.html

Scope: General and specific topics in all areas of librarianship, as well as other subjects.

History: Originated as a bulletin board for libraries, evolved into an information service for the academic and research community.

Representative links: Dozens of links of interest to serialists and librarians in general, international links to libraries (academic, public, special and school), professional library organizations. Links to many subjects other than library science are included.

20. Library of Congress.
URL: http://lcweb.loc.gov/
Scope: To provide electronic access to information from the Library of Congress.
Representative links: USMARC, LC programs and services for cataloging, acquisitions and preservation, and Z39.50, to name only a few. CONSER and CONSERline are found here as well.

21. National Library of Canada.
URL: http://www.nlc-bnc.ca/
Scope: Bilingual (English and French), serves as a source of information concerning the Library and information about Canada in general.
Date last revised: Feb. 9, 1996.
Representative links: Collections and services, publications, research, etc., of the Library, links to selected sources of information about Canada.

LIBRARY-RELATED ORGANIZATIONS

22. American Library Association.
URL: http://www.ala.org/
Scope: Information about ALA, its organization, programs, etc.
Date last revised: January 1996.
Representative links: Mostly ALA-related information, home pages for the ALA divisions, and a few links to other library-related home pages.

23. Association for Research Libraries.
URL: http://arl.cni.org/index.html
Scope: Services, projects and statistics related to ARL.
Date last revised: January 18, 1996.
Representative links: ARL projects and statistics.

24. Gabriel.

URL: http://portico.bl.uk/gabriel/en/welcome.html

Scope: Information for many of Europe's national libraries that are members of the Conference of European National Libraries (CENL), information available in English, German or French.

Representative links: Information and links to many of the national libraries of Europe; also information about CENL, its cooperative programs, membership list.

25. International Federation of Library Associations and Institutions (IFLA).

URL: http://www.nlc-bnc.ca/ifla

Scope: International.

Purpose: To provide information about IFLA, and librarianship in general.

Date last revised: February 23, 1996.

Representative links: Links to information specific to IFLA, such as conferences, publications, governance structure. Has a Virtual Library containing an extensive collection of links of interest to serialists and librarians in general, including library humor and a selection of freeware and shareware applications for libraries.

26. Taming the Serials Jungle with the ISSN (ISSN International Centre).

URL: http://www.well.com/user/issnic

Scope: The majority of this page is available in French or English.

Purpose: To supply useful information concerning the ISSN.

Representative links: Definition of ISSN, ISSN Register, ISSN and barcoding, ISSN National Centres.

27. OCLC Online Computer Library Center, Inc.

URL: http://www.oclc.org/oclc/menu/t-home1.htm

Scope: OCLC products and services.

Date last revised: April 17, 1996.

Representative links: OCLC divisions and subsidiaries, affiliated regional networks, OCLC member libraries, some links to publishers.

28. SISAC: Serials Industry Systems Advisory Committee.
URL: http://www.infor.com:80/bisg/sisac.html
Purpose: To provide a forum for the serials industry to discuss and resolve mutual concerns.
Comments: This page seems to serve as a general information source about SISAC, and thus doesn't have any links.

TECHNICAL SERVICES HOME PAGES

The following is only a sample of the many technical services home pages that can be found on the Web.

29. MIT Libraries Cataloging Oasis.
URL: http://wonder.mit.edu/cataloging.html
Scope: Local.
Date last revised: February 15, 1996.
Representative links: Useful bits of information that catalogers need on a daily basis, links to LC Marvel gopher, newsgroups and mailing lists.

30. Northwestern University Library Technical Services.
URL: http://www.library.nwu.edu:80/tech
Scope: Divided into Catalog [Department], Serials and Acquisitions Services.
Date last revised: April 17, 1996.
Representative links: Contains much local information such as procedures and staff lists. Also available is an extensive set of links to Internet resources, such as library information resources on the Internet, library journals and other information resources, library service organizations, associations, vendors, publishers and catalogs on the Internet, and reviews and other evaluating resources on the Web. Each of these headings includes many other links.

31. TPOT: Technical Processing Online Tools (University of California, San Diego).
URL: http://tpot.ucsd.edu
Scope: Local and international.
Date last revised: April 18, 1996.

Representative links: Local procedures, reports of selected meetings, contact persons, also links to the Library of Congress, OCLC, and other Internet resources.

32. University of Virginia–Cataloging Services Department.
URL: http://www.lib.virginia.edu/cataloging/
Scope: Local and national.
Date last revised: April 2, 1996.
Representative links: Procedures and local information, national newsgroups, mailing lists and electronic journals.

ALPHABETICAL INDEX OF ITEMS DESCRIBED

Readmore 16

Serials in Cyberspace: Collections, Resources, and Services 11

SERIALST Scope & Purpose 2

SISAC: Serials Industry Systems Advisory Committee 28

Taming the Serials Jungle with the ISSN (ISSN International Centre) 26

Tools for Serials Catalogers: A Collection of Useful Sites and Sources 12

TPOT: Technical Processing Online Tools (University of California, San Diego) 31

United States Book Exchange: Back Issues Shelf List 7

University of Virginia–Cataloging Services Department 32

REFERENCES

1. Ed Krol, *The Whole Internet* (Sebastopol, CA: O'Reilly & Associates, Inc., 1994), p. 509.

2. Andrew Ford, *Spinning the Web* (London: International Thomson Publishing, 1995), p. 1.

3. Marilyn Geller, Electronic mail to author, March 15, 1996.

Starting a Journal on the World Wide Web

Nancy De Sa

SUMMARY. This article discusses certain characteristics of journals published on the World Wide Web and offers guidance for those who wish to start their own journal on the Web. *[Article copies available for a fee from The Haworth Document Delivery Service: 1-800-342-9678. E-mail address: getinfo@haworth.com]*

Publishing on the Internet has become a common practice. Many people cannot make it through a day without seeing or hearing at least one Internet address for a company or organization. Although publishing on the Internet may be an intimidating prospect for some, it is actually a simple process for anyone who has the right computer hardware and something to say.

WHY PUBLISH ON THE INTERNET?

Why publish on the Internet at all? Those who publish journals in paper formats may wonder why people are rushing to publish on the Internet. One of the main reasons for this trend is that the number of people around the world who are connected to the Internet multi-

Nancy De Sa was one of the founding editors of *The Olive Tree,* a Library Science electronic journal on the Web, and served as Submissions Editor from January 1995 to August 1995.

[Haworth co-indexing entry note]: "Starting a Journal on the World Wide Web." De Sa, Nancy. Co-published simultaneously in *The Serials Librarian* (The Haworth Press, Inc.) Vol. 29, No. 3/4, 1996, pp. 189-193; and: *Serials Management in the Electronic Era: Papers in Honor of Peter Gellatly, Founding Editor of* The Serials Librarian (ed: Jim Cole, and James W. Williams) The Haworth Press, Inc., 1996, pp. 189-193. Single or multiple copies of this article are available for a fee from The Haworth Document Delivery Service [1-800-342-9678, 9:00 a.m. - 5:00 p.m. (EST). E-mail address: getinfo@ haworth.com].

plies every day. People are connecting to the Internet through online services such as America Online and CompuServe, through accounts at educational and commercial institutions, and through an increasing number of Internet service providers. Savvy publishers are taking advantage of this growing electronic audience.

Another attraction of electronic publishing is the time it removes from the traditional publishing process. Publishers no longer need to wait to send galleys to the printer or the bindery before obtaining their final product. Nor must they be concerned with distributing copies of their publication. Once a journal is prepared for presentation, it is available to anyone who is connected to the Internet. Last-minute changes or missed typographical errors no longer cause panic. Mistakes in final proofs can be fixed with a few keystrokes.

Electronic publishing also allows editors in remote locations to collaborate on the publication more easily. They can communicate with each other via electronic mail to share submitted articles instantly, and conduct real-time editorial meetings using Internet tools such as Internet Relay Chat. Editors can update and maintain the journal from remote locations by using File Transfer Protocol (FTP) to transfer revised or new articles onto the computer (or Web server) where the journal is located.

These methods of communication can also be used to communicate and share articles with the referees of journals, reducing the time needed for the review process. After editors have received articles, they can send them via electronic mail to reviewers. Once they receive articles, reviewers can either print them out or read them on-screen and then use electronic mail to send their comments back to the editors.

FEATURES OF WWW JOURNALS

Electronic publishing provides a new selection of creative layouts and designs that are not available when using a paper format. While the options for publishing a journal on the Internet include using electronic mailing lists or Gopher menus, currently the primary tool used is the World Wide Web. The Web, which incorporates the use of hypertext links, graphics, audio and video clips, provides an ideal format for electronic publishing. Using the Web, publishers can imitate the print format or expand upon it, or create entirely new formats for their journals.

Those who decide to publish on the Web should try to forget many of the restrictions that print publishing dictates. The size of the page no longer constricts layout designs or length of articles. Printing costs do not restrict the size or number of issues published. Journals no longer must be published in distinct units or issues that impose deadlines; a journal's Web presence can be added to periodically as new material is prepared. Hypertext links allow articles to be organized into separate subject areas or linked to other related articles.

A journal's home page on the Web might be presented as a table of contents that contains links to different types of articles including features, reviews, and columns. The articles might contain links not only to each other but to other information on the Internet such as the authors' personal home pages or other articles that they have written. Journals on the Web can also be connected to programs that allow readers to search for articles relating to certain keywords or written by particular authors. Graphics and audio and video clips also add a new dimension to otherwise unembellished articles. Recent developments such as the Java programming language allow the creation of dynamic Web pages that continually change as readers view them.

PREPARATION AND STORAGE OF THE TEXT

Hypertext Markup Language (HTML) must be used to prepare documents for presentation on the Web. HTML utilizes tags embedded within the text of a document to control the document's appearance. This coding is somewhat similar to that used in older word processing programs such as WordPerfect 5.1 for DOS. HTML tags such as <strong> can be used to surround text (e.g., <strong>Internet</strong>) to present words in boldface.

Many books about HTML are available at bookstores and libraries. Assistance is also available on the Internet. Refer to

http://wwwiz.com/home/cye/html.html

for an online list of books on HTML and Web publishing, or

http://www.yahoo.com/Computers_and_Internet/Software/Data_
Formats/HTML/Guides_ and_Tutorials

for an online list of Web sites that contain HTML tutorials. Refer to

http://union.ncsa.uiuc.edu/HyperNews/get/www/html/editors.html

to obtain programs known as HTML editors that provide easy-to-use graphical interfaces for creating HTML documents.

When using HTML to create Web documents, keep in mind that how individual readers view documents is determined by the Web browser that they use. Web browsers, such as Netscape and Mosaic, are graphical or textual programs that allow users to access information on the Web. Different browsers may present HTML tags differently. Because of this, it is wise, if possible, to view documents on several browsers before making them available to the public. Refer to

http://www.yahoo.com/Computers_and_Internet/Internet/World_
Wide_Web/Browsers/

for information on browsers that are available for different operating systems.

Once a document is prepared for presentation it must be placed on a Web server so that everyone who is connected to the Internet can access it. (The term server may refer to either the software or the computer on which it runs.) Since direct connections to the Internet can be costly, many publishers may want to try to locate institutions that have established servers and that are willing to allow others to use or rent space to store publications. When deciding whether to make the investment to establish a Web server or use space on someone else's, one should consider the expected number of readers and the amount of disk space that journal will use. Software needed for setting up a Web server on different operating systems is available at

http://www.yahoo.com/Computers_and_Internet/Internet/World_
Wide_Web/HTTP/Servers/

PUBLICITY

There are a variety of ways to publicize a new Web site for a journal. Two Usenet newsgroups that post announcements of new Web sites are comp.internet.net-happenings and comp.infosystems.www.announce. Comp.internet.net-happenings is also maintained as an electronic mailing list; announcements can be sent to listserv@is.internic.net. "Submit It" is a site on the Web that sends the URL (address) of new Web sites to a variety of Web catalogs that index resources that are accessible through the Web. "Submit It" is accessible at

http://www.submit-it.com

For more information for publicizing a new site on the Web, refer to

http://ep.com/faq/webannounce.html

A FINAL THOUGHT

Publishing on the Web is easier than it sounds. The best way to get started is to look at journals that are currently on the Web and see how others are using this new publishing format. There are many sites on the Web that list electronic journals. These include

http://www.lib.ncsu.edu/stacks/stacks-Scholarly.html

and

http://www.edoc.com/ejournal

New Challenges for Technical Services in the 21st Century

Nancy L. Eaton

SUMMARY. This paper forecasts changes in library technical services that are being influenced by changes in information technology, tele-communications, a transition from mass production to mass customization, and economic pressures. It predicts that technical services librarians will play new roles in organization of the World Wide Web and development of EDI technologies. The complexities of these technologies will require collaboration with other disciplines and with library networks and consortia. *[Article copies available for a fee from The Haworth Document Delivery Service: 1-800-342-9678. E-mail address: getinfo@haworth.com]*

LOOKING TOWARD THE NEXT CENTURY

In *Global Paradox,* John Naisbitt focuses on the dramatic changes taking place in information delivery and summarizes the four "big ideas" that are struggling to be realized: (1) the blending of technologies; (2) strategic alliances; (3) creating a global network; and (4) personal telecomputers for everyone.[1] He forecasts that "as the power and reach of the communications infrastructure

Nancy L. Eaton is Dean of Library Services at Iowa State University of Science and Technology, 302 Parks Library, Ames, IA 50011-2140. She has also served as chair of the OCLC Board of Trustees since 1993.

[Haworth co-indexing entry note]: "New Challenges for Technical Services in the 21st Century." Eaton, Nancy L. Co-published simultaneously in *The Serials Librarian* (The Haworth Press, Inc.) Vol. 29, No. 3/4, 1996, pp. 195-208; and: *Serials Management in the Electronic Era: Papers in Honor of Peter Gellatly, Founding Editor of* The Serials Librarian (ed: Jim Cole, and James W. Williams) The Haworth Press, Inc., 1996, pp. 195-208. Single or multiple copies of this article are available for a fee from The Haworth Document Delivery Service [1-800-342-9678, 9:00 a.m. - 5:00 p.m. (EST). E-mail address: getinfo@haworth.com].

expands, the tools needed to harness that capability shrink. They will become smaller, cheaper, lighter, and more portable. As we all become part of the greater global economy, the most efficient and effective economic unit becomes the individual."[2] He further speculates that "Telecomputing [sending and receiving voice, data, image, and video] will become thoroughly decentralized, completely individualized, and will, among other things, further erode the centralized character of corporate giants that grew out of the industrial era as they give way to loose federations of small entrepreneurial-like companies."[3] Nicholas Negroponte, in *being digital,* also forecasts changes based upon the power of the individual to access information, projecting that "In the post-information age, we often have an audience the size of one. Everything is made to order, and information is extremely personalized."[4] Along with the technological changes that are giving individuals increasing power to define how they wish to access information, there is an increasing emphasis within management theory on quality improvement that focuses on client-defined needs. In addition, many organizations, both public and private, are competing to provide information resources to the same clientele packaged in ways they want it. These trends will place significant pressure on libraries to respond to individuals' expectations on how they wish to access information.

In *Mass Customization,* Pine describes a profound shift taking place in many aspects of life: "mass customization," or the production and distribution of *customized* goods and services on a *mass* scale. He sees this phenomenon taking place both in the computing industry and in the telecommunications industry. Pine describes how these industries now provide standardized technology with many options built in that allow the client or customer to tailor its usage to a great degree.[5] Pine's description of the transition from mass production to highly customizable products provides an explanation of how this trend toward individualized information delivery will work in practice. As libraries increasingly use computing and networks to deliver information, the way information is packaged will change and will allow users to select when, where, and how they wish to access and receive that information.

Adaptations by publishers to provide scholarly publications in a networked environment are starting to change the way some publications are packaged. Publishers are very concerned about losing revenues from existing publications as they move into the electronic publishing environment. Pricing mechanisms and revisions to editing, production, and archiving methods are in transition and hard to predict, but some trends are emerging. Simultaneously, the decline in purchasing power by libraries is resulting in a renewed focus on improved interlibrary loan and document delivery systems as alternatives to purchasing, resulting in the new focus on "access" as an alternative to "ownership" in recent collection development literature.

In addition, the effects of public pressure for tax reductions and reductions in the federal debt, combined with continuing high inflation rates in the publishing industry, are forcing all libraries to search for more economical and efficient ways to carry out their missions. Statistics from the Association of Research Libraries substantiate that even with significant increases in funding for purchase of library materials in the last decade, the percentage of published titles purchased annually by research libraries continues to decrease, at the same time that demand for services continues to increase while staffing has not.[6]

These themes are mutually reinforcing, resulting in a convergence of pressures for change that are directly affecting the functions and even the mission of libraries. Libraries are subject to the trend of "mass customization," and technical services librarians will be challenged to reformulate bibliographic control in this environment. They will also be challenged to find more efficient ways to accomplish current activities in order to reallocate staff to meet these new challenges.

FROM LOCAL SYSTEMS TO NETWORKED RESOURCES

Until recently, the role of technical services was to acquire, organize, and make accessible those materials being purchased by a library. During the decades of the 1970s and 1980s, technical services focused upon the transition from manual systems to shared network utilities and local automated systems, and utilization of automated vendor systems as vendors also made the transition from manual to automated systems within their own companies. With the advent of online cataloging and the emergence of online public access catalogs, catalog departments found themselves implementing electronic versions of card catalog and authority maintenance. Emphasis has been to catalog on one of several national databases, to add those records to the utility, and to download those records to the local system in order to update the local catalog database. Public access was from dedicated terminals on dedicated lines due to constraints of point-to-point telecommunications configurations. With the advent of wide area networks and local area networks, that constraint has disappeared; and access by users from personal workstations anywhere on the network is an increasing expectation.

By contrast, public services units were using commercial networks to access commercial indexing/abstracting databases. With the advent of CD-ROM technology in the mid-1980s, libraries began to mount CD-ROM indexing/abstracting databases on local workstations in order to lower the unit cost of searching, since the library could subscribe to the database on an annual basis as if it were a serial subscription. As library automation vendors added capabilities to online catalogs, allowing libraries to load these indexing/abstracting databases onto the local library system for access via local campus or library networks, the distinction between catalogs and indexing/abstracting databases began to blur. Where vendors such as NOTIS developed linkages between the indexing/abstracting database citation and the local catalog of the library's actual holdings, the distinction blurred even further. Again, distributed access from wide area networks or local area networks from personal computers has become increasingly common and desired.

The user, however, still wants the actual article or book or piece of information. For the user, these tools are only the first step in actual information delivery. Recent emphasis on document delivery and movement by some publishers to change their production systems to facilitate article delivery finally may allow libraries to integrate the finding tools with actual information delivery. There are specific examples of this beginning to take place:

1. *Interlibrary loan enhancements*: An important change taking place in interlibrary loan operations is a new distinction between "returnables" and "non-returnables." Generally a "returnable" is

a monograph that does not lend itself to photocopying or digitizing of an article or chapter. A "non-returnable" is an article or book chapter that lends itself to photocopying or digitizing or faxing; use of these technologies to distribute publications reduces labor and postage costs for mailing the piece in two directions and may also allow for the item to be sent directly to the individual rather than to the library, since the library does not have to take responsibility for the return of the piece. With the ability to send digited images or telefacsimile copies to a workstation, the distribution of "non-returnables" will become increasingly electronic as costs for distribution over networks become cheaper than the costs of postage and labor to package and mail the piece. As more users have workstations with these capabilities, networked distribution also has the advantage that the piece can be routed directly to the user's workstation. Billing, if there are associated costs, can be independent of the receiving site.

2. *Patron-initiated interlibrary loan/document delivery*: Many libraries are instituting electronic mail or Internet-based "forms" systems that allow a patron to search, find a citation, and request the item online utilizing the citation. The request is routed to an interlibrary loan or document delivery service unit for action, though there is increasing interest in automating the entire process and eliminating human intervention by library staff.

3. *Full-text electronic publications*: The ARL directory of electronic journals[7] documents the growth in full-text journals available electronically. In addition, a number of publishers including Elsevier and the Association of Computing Machinery (ACM) are converting their journal production systems to electronic format. This will facilitate the ability to search and locate specific publications and to request electronic document delivery at the article or chapter level. In addition, many users and organizations are creating home pages and mounting full text publications that are accessible via the Internet.

4. *Electronic warehouses and archives*: Increasingly the publishing process is being changed so that the publisher uses a database as the basic storage medium, with different output formats based upon distribution methods. For example, Elsevier Science Publishing is redesigning its entire editorial and production system to create an

electronic storehouse from which the publisher can produce any combination of output media: electronic full text online, microform, CD-ROM, or paper. Using an electronic warehouse also allows the publisher to update the central database constantly, thus reducing delays in making a publication available.

5. *Multimedia formats*: One of Naisbitt's four "big ideas" is the blending of technologies, incorporating voice, data, image, and video into new multimedia information products and publications. Similar to the linkages between citations and full text articles described above, the MARC-II cataloging format now contains an 856 field that can be used to link to multimedia publications and allow the users to download the item to their own workstations. There is considerable debate within the library and computing communities as to whether the MARC-II communication format and traditional cataloging are adequate to the needs of the future or whether a new approach expanding on cataloging concepts will be necessary. This is a common discussion item at meetings of the Coalition for Networked Information, a coalition of members of the Association of Research Libraries, CAUSE, and Educom. Whatever the specific technical formats used to accomplish these linkages, the direction is clear. Thus, as with journal articles, the cataloging not only describes the publication but now allows for automated retrieval from the citation. This trend is bound to continue as libraries provide for additional formats such as maps, satellite data, statistical databases, etc. For users, the citation is only the first step in accomplishing their larger objective, which is to retrieve the information or publication.

These trends point to the likelihood that the physical volume or issue of a journal will give way to databases with individual articles that can be located through powerful search engines searching citation databases, linking the article by ISSN (or other equivalent identification number at the issue level) to local library holdings and/or external document delivery services, and with the possibility of distribution either to the user's workstation or to the library.

The distinction between locally owned and remotely accessible information may blur further if publisher licenses allow libraries the option of mounting the electronic subscription locally or archiving it with a third party, making possible the linking of local and remote holdings for the same title. It would appear to be economically desirable for libraries to mount current and/or heavily used data on local systems but to rely on a third party such as the publisher, a state or regional consortium, a national network such as OCLC or RLG, or a vendor such as EBSCO, for the backfiles as the data become less used, in order to reduce the storage costs. Whether the data are held locally or remotely can be hidden from the user, with the search and retrieval technicalities imbedded in the software that supports the systems. For this to be practical, publishers and librarians will have to deal with the challenges of electronic archiving, licensing issues, and fairly complex financial and copyright tracking systems.

NETWORK TOOLS VERSUS TRADITIONAL CATALOGING

The trend toward mass customization of information is being facilitated by several key factors: (1) use of technical standards to allow vendors to design customized information products based upon standard information and telecommunication formats; (2) networks, particularly the explosive growth of the Internet, as common carriers for scholarly communication; (3) increased reliance on purchase of vendor software or network services and products that provide for many options that can be selected by the library or patron; and (4) the increase in use of client/server architecture in which the provision of the information on a "server" is separated from the "client" or access software. Increasingly, client software is available from competing vendors that provide special features targeted to niche market client needs but with common retrieval standards such as the Z39.50 retrieval standard incorporated into the client code. Thus, the user can select the client software of choice, based upon the special features in the retrieval software, so long as the source data are stored using accepted data formats, such as the MARC-II communications format, independent of the retrieval method.

The influence of the Internet on the future of information technology is enormous. Its rapid growth is a true phenomenon. Because of its general acceptance worldwide, the National Science Foundation has invested heavily in the development of NIDR (Networked Information Discovery and Retrieval) tools. Early Web tools such as Gopher, Archie, and Veronica have been surpassed by Mosaic and most recently Netscape and Java. Microsoft has announced that it will market a competitor to Netscape as a network browser. Just as CD-ROM technology in the information industry was driven by its mass entertainment audio CD predecessor, retrieval tools used by libraries will be driven by the browsers and client software from the mass market due to the amount of corporate money available for research and development that is not available within the academic or library communities. In addition, the complexities of these technologies surpass what the library field can develop on its own. Thus, collaborations and partnerships are increasingly necessary for libraries to remain major participants in the evolution of storage and retrieval technologies. A result of this trend is that librarians will have to adapt tools being developed by other disciplines; but we should try to influence the development of those tools, as we have a great deal of experience with the organization of information and how people use it. Increasingly that experience is being recognized by such organizations as the Coalition for Networked Information.

The inability to control what is on the Internet at any given moment significantly changes the approaches that must be used to organize information on it, as compared to the more controlled environment of the online public access catalog which describes items actually owned and controlled by the library. The increasing availability of multimedia formats that can be retrieved and delivered to a workstation over the Internet also provides new challenges to librarians about how to work the new formats and the retrieval mechanisms into cataloging systems. There is ongoing debate whether the MARC-II communications format is still viable in this environment or whether other formats need to replace it. The probability is that additional data formats will be used in addition to the MARC-II format, such as the various formats for images, flat files for full-text data, relational database formats, etc. Librarians will need to learn more about these other formats and their uses, as well as how to translate data from one format to another (e.g., relational database formats to the MARC-II format, and vice versa), just as programs now exist that convert from one word-processing format to another.

ACADEMIC PRODUCTIVITY IMPROVEMENTS

Higher education is under great pressure to find ways of cost containment due to the high inflation index for higher education and for libraries, as compared to the general inflation index, and due to the concern for reducing the national deficit and lowering taxes. Current buzzwords are "reallocation" and "doing more with less." This is also the reason for growing attention to "continuous quality improvement" efforts on campuses, an effort to apply Total Quality Management (TQM) concepts to not-for-profit or public institutions in order to utilize resources in ways that are directed to the "client." Many universities are trying to implement versions of TQM, as are research libraries. The Association of Research Libraries has built continuous quality improvement concepts into its training programs, and libraries such as Oregon State University and University of Arizona are illustrations of ongoing efforts in the library environment. When this author appeared before the Iowa Board of Regents to submit the Inter-institutional Library Report for the three regents university libraries (the University of Iowa, Iowa State University of Science and Technology, and University of Northern Iowa) at its December 1995 meeting, board members clearly articulated that the three libraries must continue to cooperate as part of cost containment, that information technology was a strategic direction for the Board of Regents, and that reallocation of resources was one expectation for funding of information technology.[8]

In a recent issue of *Educom Review,* Massy and Zemsky discuss the potential conflict when using information technology for academic productivity improvements.

> Most discussions of the possible advantages of IT-based teaching and learning strategies start off weighing the relative advantage of technology against the inherent capabilities of faculty. What can IT contribute to increasing learning productivity? First, IT offers economies of scale: After a (sometimes large) front-end investment, the cost of usage per incremental

cost per incremental student is apt to be low. Moreover, access to very large amounts of information can be obtained at low incremental cost . . . IT also offers mass customization–faculty can accommodate individual differences in student goals, learning styles and abilities, while providing improved convenience for both the students and faculty on an "any time, any place" basis. These propositions add up to a "modern industrial revolution." But whereas the original industrial revolution led to undifferentiated mass-production outputs, the modern information-driven revolution permits production to be adapted to the needs of each customer.[9]

Massy and Zemsky go on to state that:

Using IT for "more-with-less" productivity enhancements requires that technology replace some activities now being performed by faculty, teaching assistants and support personnel. With labor accounting for 70 percent or more of current operating costs, there simply is no other way . . . Faculty will need to invest time and energy in learning about what they do and why they do it, and then open themselves to the possibility of doing things differently.

In looking at the trade-offs, they indicate that "Using information technology to enhance productivity will increase the ratio of capital to labor cost in the academic budget, whether or not overall costs can be reduced. Large capital-labor ratios represent a shift away from the handicraft mentality and offer several advantages."

These same economic arguments apply to libraries. Library directors regularly talk about the pressure to reallocate staff from technical services to public services. OCLC has developed products that allow libraries to contract out increasing numbers of functions in technical services; and OCLC is now partnering with publishers to automate acquisitions to a higher degree so that the book comes shelf ready from point of order. A further improvement that would aid the publisher, supplier, library, and university accounting offices would be the implementation of electronic fund transfers using national standards for Electronic Data Interchange (EDI).[10] The need for productivity enhancements to allow libraries to do "more with less" will force these changes, given static or shrinking budgets that cannot keep up with either labor costs or inflation for journals and monographs. To the extent that technical services librarians are seen to be contributing their expertise to the development of new NIDR tools or to productivity improvements in the business functions of acquisitions, they will remain valued. To the extent that they are viewed as perpetuating systems that are no longer cost-effective, they will be vulnerable to replacement, since other methods now can be found to do some of the work currently performed by librarians. Even if those methods are problematic, they will be employed in order to shift human resources to other areas of the library that have direct user demand.

POTENTIAL TECHNICAL SERVICES CONTRIBUTIONS

It is very important that catalogers and acquisitions specialists recognize the need to recast their skills to address a new set of problems facing the organization and management of information in libraries, specifically the challenges of organizing information in a distributed networked environment and the need for productivity improvements. They have important expertise to bring to bear on these problems; but this expertise may need to be reconceptualized. For instance, catalogers have invaluable expertise in bibliographic description for complex publications. This expertise transfers to the description of new forms of information such as multimedia formats, satellite data, geographic information system (GIS) data, etc. Once linkages are made in online public access catalogs or library home pages to sources on the Internet, it is important to keep those linkages current. OCLC is experimenting with software that would check linkages and generate reports if linkages are not found; technical services librarians might play a role in processing those error reports and contributing to a new version of database maintenance.

Similarly, acquisitions specialists have invaluable knowledge about the business functions within libraries and within their parent institutions. They need to be involved in the design of new EDI applications and methods and in the creation of order and payment systems for electronic formats or document delivery options for materials that are not necessarily received by the library directly.

They also need to be involved in the development of systems that track transactions between libraries and that minimize local billing or invoicing.

Specifically, technical services librarians need to be focusing on two types of needs within libraries and the information industry: (1) bibliographic and retrieval tools for information that is distributed across national and international networks and may change constantly; and (2) changes in acquisitions and fund accounting, with further integration of workflow between acquisitions and cataloging functions and use of EDI standards to facilitate electronic transfer of ordering and fiscal information. Key issues for bibliographic control and NIDR technology include the changeability of the information in a networked environment (both the location of the information and the source data), the increasing number of formats that librarians must deal with, and complications for authority control as new tools rely increasingly on keyword searching. Key issues in acquisitions include the implementation of EDI standards, further coordination across systems (library, parent institution, vendor), the need to create fiscal controls on orders for material or information which may never be received physically by the library, the need for fund allocation systems for electronic information at the level of the individual as well as the department, and the need for much richer management data than is currently available.

PARTNERSHIPS AND ALLIANCES

Given the complexity of the technologies libraries are now required to utilize, librarians must collaborate with other disciplines and within their own consortia and networks to be successful. The expertise needed to tame these technologies and make them work for us lies in library science, computer science, management information systems, and within the subject expertise of the specialists who utilize information. Thus, librarians increasingly must partner with organizations outside the library to be effective. Collective action is much more likely to succeed than isolated individual actions. The second of Naisbitt's four major trends is "strategic alliances." Consequently, we see increasing evidence of research and development efforts by library consortia (such as OCLC, the Research Libraries Group, and Ohionet) on behalf of libraries. Research and demonstration projects such as the six digital library grants funded by NSF/ARPA/NASA also combine the knowledge and skills of several disciplines.[11] Partnerships and collaborations will focus on development of technical standards that facilitate open platforms, client/server architecture, development of NIDR tools, and implementation of discipline-based electronic publications and databases. Because the environment is still quite changeable, there also will be demonstration projects among libraries, networks, and publishers that explore new service and economic models. Examples of these include the digital libraries projects, the Red Sage Project at the University of California at San Francisco which focuses on medical literature, and the OCLC/Elsevier test sites which will focus on implementation of full text electronic journals in the sciences by libraries such as Iowa State University and University of Toronto.

CONCLUSIONS

Naisbitt, Negroponte, Pine, Massy, and Zemsky provide a very consistent forecast of the future in which mass production and centralization will give way to mass customization, decentralization, and networked communications. Increasingly catalog librarians will need to utilize their skills to produce bibliographic descriptions for a much wider range of materials that may be owned by the library or accessed from remote servers residing anywhere on the Internet, utilizing data formats that can reside on servers independent of the client software selected by the user for retrieval and manipulation. They may have a new role to play with maintaining linkages between library catalogs or home pages and resources residing on servers on the Internet. Acquisitions librarians will need to focus on EDI formats, close coordination of workflow between acquisitions and cataloging, and better management reports; these efforts are aimed at increasing productivity not only within the library but also within the parent institution and within the vendor systems. This will require collaboration with other disciplines and within library consortia, given the complexity of the information and computing technologies being employed.

REFERENCES

1. John Naisbitt. *Global Paradox* (New York: Avon Books, 1995, c1994), 62-63.

2. Naisbitt, 64.

3. Naisbitt, 63.

4. Nicholas Negroponte. *being digital* (New York: Knopf, 1995), 164.

5. B. Joseph Pine II. *Mass Customization: The New Frontier in Business Competition* (Boston: Harvard Business School Press, 1993), x, 36-38.

6. *ARL Statistics, 1993-94.* Compiled by Martha Kyrillidou, Kaylyn E. Hipps, and Kendon Stubbs. (Washington, DC: Association of Research Libraries, 1995), 5-13.

7. *Directory of Electronic Journals, Newsletters, and Academic Discussion Lists.* Edited by Ann Okerson (Washington, DC: Association of Research Libraries, Office of Scientific and Academic Publishing, 1994).

8. Nancy L. Eaton. Testimony before the Iowa Board of Regents. Des Moines, IA, December 13, 1995.

9. William F. Massy and Robert Zemsky. "Information Technologies and Academic Productivity," *Educom Review* 31/1 (January/February 1996): 12-14.

10. Sandra K. Paul. "Open EDI, Interactive EDI, and More EDI on the Internet," *Against the Grain* (April, 1994): 62.

11. For descriptions of the six digital library projects, see: (1) Gary Stix. "The Speed of Write," *Scientific American* 271, no. 6 (December 1994): 106-111; and (2) Paul Evans Peters. "Digital Libraries Are Much More Than Digitized Collections," *Educom Review* 30/4 (July/August 1995): 11-15.

Not Just E-Journals:
Providing and Maintaining Access
to Serials and Serial Information
Through the World-Wide Web

Robert D. Cameron

SUMMARY. The Directory of Computing Science Journals is being developed as a prototype for Internet serials directories accessible through the World-Wide Web. Each entry in the directory consists of a web page providing basic journal information and a comprehensive collection of links to known Internet-based resources related to the journal. Design goals for the directory are to provide a comprehensive, reliable, efficient, authoritative and up-to-date information resource for computing science journals. Particular emphasis has been placed on proactive maintenance techniques for correction and enhancement of the link collections. *[Article copies available for a fee from The Haworth Document Delivery Service: 1-800-342-9678. E-mail address: getinfo@haworth.com]*

INTRODUCTION

A model World-Wide Web resource for serials entitled the "Directory of Computing Science Journals" (URL http://elib.cs.

Robert D. Cameron is affiliated with the School of Computing Science, Simon Fraser University, Burnaby, British Columbia, Canada V5A 156 (E-mail: cameron@cs.sfu.ca).

[Haworth co-indexing entry note]: "Not Just E-Journals: Providing and Maintaining Access to Serials and Serial Information Through the World-Wide Web." Cameron, Robert D. Co-published simultaneously in *The Serials Librarian* (The Haworth Press, Inc.) Vol. 29, No. 3/4, 1996, pp. 209-222; and: *Serials Management in the Electronic Era: Papers in Honor of Peter Gellatly, Founding Editor of The Serials Librarian* (ed: Jim Cole, and James W. Williams) The Haworth Press, Inc., 1996, pp. 209-222. Single or multiple copies of this article are available for a fee from The Haworth Document Delivery Service [1-800-342-9678, 9:00 a.m. - 5:00 p.m. (EST). E-mail address: getinfo@haworth.com].

sfu.ca/cs-journals/ on the Web) is currently under development as one component of the Internet Electronic Library project at Simon Fraser University. In contrast to most virtual or electronic libraries now extant on the Web, this directory provides access to information about both electronic and print journals. Currently, the directory contains information pages for more than 400 journals of interest to computer scientists, a larger collection for this subject than one would typically find in all but the most comprehensive of research libraries. As such, it may be a good model for the development of directories of serials for other disciplines and perhaps ultimately a comprehensive multidisciplinary directory of serials.

Each page in the journal directory provides information on one academic journal. As could be expected in any serials catalog, this includes basic information such as the journal title, ISSN and publisher. Using the hypertext capabilities of the Web, however, the remainder of each page is designed to provide access to a variety of information sources and services related to the journal. In most cases, the first of these is a set of hypertext links to known information servers operated by the publisher. In this way, even if there are problems with the reliability, authoritativeness or currency of other information resources on the page, the user always has access to whatever information is available directly from the source. Most academic society and commercial journal publishers now operate at least a Web server, many operate gopher and FTP servers as well and perhaps also separate servers from various international offices; links to each of these are provided in order to increase reliability and efficiency of access. In addition to top-level access to the publishers' servers, the directory also includes direct access to pages within the server information hierarchies that provide any specific information related to the journal, for example, an entry in an on-line journal catalog, an on-line "title page" for the journal or a journal "home page" on the Web. In most cases, publishers are now making tables of contents and sometimes abstracts available; links to theme resources are also included.

Beyond publisher-provided information about a journal, links to information from other sources are included as well. Often, a "home page" for a journal may be maintained separately from the publisher by the journal's editor-in-chief. These pages frequently have information not found on publisher's catalog pages, such as information about the reviewing backlog, special issues that are being contemplated and so on. There are also sources of information completely independent of the journal's publication. In particular, there are many independent on-line bibliographic resources for journals; and in some cases there are several sources for a given journal in various different formats. Links to each of these are included, so long as there is at least some evidence of a well-maintained bibliographic collection over a significant period of time. Other sources of information that may be included on the page include access to document delivery services and libraries. At present, there are links to the CARL UnCover and CISTI document delivery services for any journal held in their respective collections (using ISSN matching as a key). As an initial experiment in access to library holdings information, the directory also provides link to the SFU OPAC through its WWW interface. This works well and gives information about specific holdings in the SFU journal collection. Ultimately, the goal is to provide links for holdings information in most significant libraries and library consortia.

Figure 1 shows a screen snapshot of an sample information page from the Directory, as captured using a standard web browser. The page collects together basic information about the journal and includes ten hypertext links to information sources (links are shown underlined). These include top-level links to three information servers operated by the publisher and one by the sponsoring organization. A publisher's title page and a sponsor's home page for the journal are also provided. Links to an independently-maintained bibliographic database for the journal are provided, both to the originating site at the University of Utah and to a mirrored copy of it at Simon Fraser University. For ordering articles from the journal, a link to the CARL UnCover service is provided. Finally, a link to Simon Fraser University's OPAC is used to provide local holdings information.

Although the Directory of Computing Science Journals is being developed as a practical resource useful in its own right, its primary role is as a research prototype for exploring a variety of issues in the development of Internet electronic libraries. Section 2 discusses

FIGURE 1. Page for "Computing Systems" in the Directory of Computing Science Journals

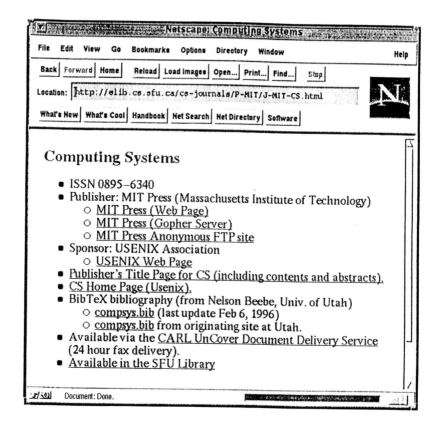

design criteria for web pages in Internet electronic libraries and how those criteria apply to Internet serials directories. One of the most important criteria is the maintenance of reliable and up-to-date access to Internet resources; Section 3 goes on to discuss this issue and some of the successful techniques and technologies employed in the computing science journals directory. Section 4 concludes the paper with a brief discussion of future directions for Internet serials directories.

DESIGN PHILOSOPHY FOR WEB PAGES
WITHIN INTERNET ELECTRONIC LIBRARIES

One objective in developing the Directory of Computing Science Journals has been to explore design philosophies for web pages and hierarchies as components of an Internet electronic library. The overall goal of an Internet electronic library should be to bring organization to the Web in order to provide users consistent access to high-quality information resources. But what does this mean? It should mean that the web pages within an Internet electronic library seek to meet at least the following criteria in providing access to information:

1. Authoritativeness and currency of information.
2. Comprehensiveness within a well-defined focus.
3. Integrated access to print and electronic resources.
4. Efficiency and reliability.

The role of each of these criteria in web page design is discussed below and illustrated in particular application to Internet serials directories.

Authoritativeness and currency of information. A great advantage of the Web for serials directories and other library applications is the possibility of including direct links to original sources for access to authoritative and current information. In particular, linking directly to information servers operated by publishers can provide access to authoritative and current bibliographic information such as publication history, frequency of publication, etc. This can greatly simplify the serials cataloging process: why copy information from a journal issue when you can link to the on-line title page instead? Even if it is deemed desirable to enter some of this information directly into the serials catalog, links to the publisher's servers provide an important role in allowing users to confirm the accuracy and currency of catalog information. In general, it is a recommended principle of Internet electronic library development that the first step in incorporating any item into the collection is to link to the original source.[1]

Ultimately, it would also be quite useful to have access to authoritative bibliographic information by sources independent of the publishers. Ideally, authoritative ISSN information and other basic publication data could be provided by direct links to the ISSN International Centre (http://www.well.com/user/issnic). Unfortunately, the appropriate Internet access to individual serial information is not available at this time. Another possibility may eventually be to provide access to authoritative information from an appropriate cooperative or consortium of academic libraries, such as CONSER (http://lcweb.loc.gov/acq/conser/homepage.html).

One drawback of a serials catalog heavily dependent on Internet links for access to information is that links are frequently "broken" by changes in access protocols. Techniques and technologies for link maintenance are discussed in Section 3 of this paper.

Comprehensiveness within a well-defined focus. The idea here is that each web page or hierarchy should have a well-defined focus or purpose and attempt to be comprehensive within that focus. Knowing the focus of a page a user should be able to judge the suitability of the page for his or her needs. Having selected a page with an appropriate focus, a user should be able to trust that the page will provide access to any Internet-accessible information on the desired topic. The user should also be able to trust negative results; failure to find information through the page should be a strong indication that the information is not available through the Internet.

For Internet serials directories, the most important implication of comprehensiveness is that entries within a directory should be comprehensive information pages for serials and not just links to journal home pages. As discussed in the introduction, there may be a number of independent information sources for a particular journal in addition to the publisher's servers. These include editor home pages, pages of sponsoring organizations, bibliographic collections, document delivery sources and conventional library catalogs with holdings information. For comprehensiveness, an information page in the serials directory should strive to provide access to information about the serial from every reasonable information source that exists. A journal home page may or may not provide access to such resources, for a variety of reasons. In particular, some information sources may contain review information not favorable to a particular journal or publisher or alternative access to articles not in the publisher's economic interest; it seems unlikely that a publisher would link to these. If an Internet electronic library strives to provide independent comprehensive access to journal information, it cannot discharge this responsibility simply by linking to journal home pages.

From the user perspective, comprehensiveness allows users to choose from competing information resources whenever they exist. For example, databases of journal article citations may be available from a number of sources. The publisher's server may provide the most up-to-date information, possibly even with titles of accepted articles yet to appear. A bibliographic collection in BibTeX format may be convenient for users wishing to include references in documents formatted using the LATEX software system, while a *refer* format may be convenient for users of *troff.* In other cases, users may wish to use searchable bibliographies, perhaps with hypertext links on author names as in the Hypertext Bibliography Project.[2]

A second application of the notion of comprehensiveness within a well-defined focus is in identifying the particular journal set to be included in a directory. For example, the focus of the "Directory of Computing Science Journals" is serials of academic interest from a computing science perspective. In order to be comprehensive, a rather liberal view is taken of the terms "academic" and "computing science." Ideally, every journal with at least some significant academic interest from a computing science perspective would be included in the collection. Of course, one should expect that a research prototype is not likely to achieve this ideal, but it is nevertheless the goal.

Integrated access to print and electronic materials. As a further application of the idea of comprehensiveness, Internet serials directories should attempt to provide integrated access to both print and electronic materials. This argues against the commonplace practice within Internet electronic libraries of creating serials directories that focus on electronic serials only. Although casual users of an Internet electronic library may only be interested in information that they can obtain directly on-line, serious users will be happy to find on-line information directing them to appropriate paper-based resources as well.

There may be some thought that directories of electronic journals somehow give prominence to this new form of publication as a proactive contribution to reform in scholarly communication.[3] However, with the preponderance of academic material still being published on paper, the effect is likely the reverse. Serious literature research will still begin with resources that provide access to the bulk of the literature published on paper; resources that provide access to electronic publications only will be used as an afterthought, if at all. Thus a greater contribution to the promotion of electronic journals is to provide Internet-based literature resources that provide integrated access to journal publications of all forms.

Efficiency and reliability. In addition to providing access to information, it is highly desirable that the access be efficient and reliable. This is a serious challenge for Internet electronic libraries for a variety of reasons. Remote information servers may be accessible to a particular client only through low-speed communication links. A server itself may be overloaded or otherwise slow to respond. Reliability may be compromised by network failures anywhere along the path from client to server and back. Links may also fail because of modifications to information hierarchies or access protocols at the servers.

Providing redundant access to information is one step that can help alleviate both efficiency and reliability problems. One way of doing this is through the identification and/or implementation of Internet *mirror* sites. In Internet terminology, a *mirror* is an archive at one network site that faithfully reproduces an original archive at another site. The mirror site is constantly updated to ensure that it always reflects the current state of the original archive. (Of course, this discussion applies only to those materials whose copyright conditions specifically allow copying and redistribution.) Mirrors are useful to provide an efficient means of access to clients that are "electronically closer" to the mirror site than to the original archive. Mirrors also provide greater reliability: an alternative source for the material when the original archive is unavailable. Mirroring can be supported by software that automatically tracks changes at originating sites or by manual procedures regularly applied.

Identifying and linking to existing mirror sites is thus a key activity in creating efficient and reliable access to information resources within an Internet electronic library. In the case of a serials directory, for example, many journals (especially electronic ones) now provide alternative home pages on geographically dispersed servers. These alternative home pages increase the reliability and convenience of access to the journal and links to each such page should be included within the directory. In a similar fashion, different international offices of a publisher may operate servers that mirror journal catalog information; separate links to each of these sites should be included as well.

It is also quite reasonable for an Internet electronic library to implement its own mirrors for selected materials (provided that the necessary permissions are in place, of course). At present, the Directory of Computing Science Journals mirrors several good collections of (free) bibliographic data related to computing science journals. Other mirroring projects and technologies are under development.

Another form of redundancy is to provide access to alternative information resources of overlapping functionality. For example, titles of published journal articles may be available from several sources in different formats, as mentioned previously. This not only provides users with flexibility in choosing the format and organization of the information, it also provides valuable alternative sources when efficiency or reliability problems beset a user's primary choice.

Redundancy is a good strategy to deal with temporary failures in accessing remote servers, but it must be complemented with a maintenance process to deal with any permanent changes in access protocol. Consideration of this issue is the topic of the next section.

PROACTIVE MAINTENANCE FOR CORRECTION AND ENHANCEMENT IN INTERNET ELECTRONIC LIBRARIES

An unfortunate fact of life for creators of Internet electronic libraries is that links to documents and services at other sites need regular maintenance to ensure that they are up to date. Internet links are often dependent on several attributes, typically including a protocol (e.g., http, gopher or ftp) for accessing the item, an Internet address for the computer (server) which provides the item in question, a port number at which the server listens to requests using the given protocol and a local filename, pathname, or other string that the server uses to retrieve the specific item in question. For example, the *universal resource locators* (URLs) used to make links in the World-Wide Web are essentially notations for specifying such attribute combinations in a form which allows unambiguous retrieval of an item.[4] Unfortunately, this means that installed links in an Internet electronic library will need to be updated whenever any one of its attributes changes. Reasons for such changes seem frequent and varied: reorganization of material to a new structure, moving information to a better maintained or more powerful server, switchover from one protocol to another for providing information, and so forth. Even though most serious information providers attempt to provide relatively stable access to their resources, in the present context of the Internet, "stability" may mean no more than one or two years without change. At present, then, Internet librarians must expect to make corrections to a significant percent of installed links each month.

One relatively passive method for monitoring links is to solicit feedback about broken links or other problems directly from the users. Many electronic libraries include e-mail contact addresses to report problems in a top-level menu. It may be more valuable to include a "feedback" selection with every menu or information page, so that it is immediately visible to the user whenever an error occurs. Indeed, the top-level directory of a library may not be directly accessible to a user who has accessed a submenu through an external link or as the result of a search. It is now fairly common to find WWW servers with contact addresses on every information page.

A much better approach to monitoring, though, is to employ a proactive process of routinely checking all the external links within a link collection. While tedious, it is possible to do this manually. However, it is also possible to automate the process with link-checking programs that exhaustively test every link. Care should be taken in using such programs because of the potentially high volume of network traffic they can generate. At present there are several rudimentary programs available for performing link-checking on the Web; the best of these is probably the MOMspider utility.[5]

Unfortunately, link-checking programs need to undergo further development before they are really ready for everyday application in the maintenance of Internet electronic libraries. One problem is that most of these programs–including MOMspider–only check *http* links, ignoring other Internet protocols such as *gopher* and *ftp*. A second problem is that they do not deal well with link "families": collections of links to different files within a common directory structure. The existing link-checking programs generate considerable unnecessary network traffic by checking every family member every time the program is run. A third problem is that error reporting and error follow-up are often not good. For example, if a link fails because of a time-out condition, automatic retesting of the link at a later time would be appropriate, but none of the existing link-checkers do this. Development of an improved second-generation link-checking program is one of the current goals of the Internet Electronic Library Project at SFU.

Link-checking and correction is only the first half of the maintenance issue for Internet electronic libraries. Even if the existing links in a collection are well-maintained, a collection can go rapidly out of date if a regular effort is not made to enhance the collection with relevant new items as they become available on the Internet. Recently, some automated tools to assist in acquiring new links for the computing science journal directory have been used to good effect. In essence, these tools are based on automatic monitoring of selected information pages at various sites on the Web. This monitoring process downloads pages when they change and then compares the new pages with their older versions. In this way, added or deleted links are automatically brought to our attention. These tools are similar in concept to others under development elsewhere.[6]

This process has been implemented for a few dozen web pages relevant to the computing science journals collection. Many of the pages monitored are publishers' index pages to the complete sets of journals they publish. This allows the automatic acquisition of links to new journals as soon as they appear in the web pages of any of the monitored publishers. Index pages of some notable bibliographic collections are also monitored for any new items they might provide. Finally, a few monitors have been installed for related

Internet electronic library pages that include computing science journal information.

These monitoring processes have been in place for only a short time, but are proving quite successful. By comparing the differences between new and old versions of an information page, it is usually very easy to identify new links to add to a collection. This monitoring process is also proving quite useful in link correction. In particular, a publisher may make wholesale changes to the organization of its Web server that results in breaking of every link to its journals within a library collection. A link checker like MOMspider finds all these broken links and reports them, but is not much help beyond that. Using the monitored page data, however, it may be possible to quickly correct all the links through a straightforward comparison of the new and old versions of the publisher's index pages. This has proven to be the case in at least two instances in the maintenance of the computing science journals directory.

Development of automatic monitoring techniques and software is a topic of continuing interest at SFU. One direction for this work is to model the information sources in a way that distinguishes between relevant and irrelevant information on a monitored page. For example, some of the changes that may be encountered in monitored documents consist only of formatting changes: using revised layouts and/or fonts without changing the basic information. Another example is a statement on a publisher's web page that says that the page is current as of a particular date. On a regularly maintained page, the publisher may change the date with each review of the information contained therein, but the change is irrelevant to link monitoring and acquisition unless the information itself changes.

A second direction for development of monitoring software is to attempt automatic incorporation of changes into the information hierarchy. Using monitoring software only, changes must be made manually after reviewing the differences between old and new versions of monitored documents. Again, the approach may be to consider an information *model* for the source document; new information that is added in a fashion consistent with this model can presumably be added automatically to the journal database. It seems reasonable to submit these changes to a manual verification process before making them, but it should nevertheless speed up incorporation of changes from monitored information sources.

Of course, software tools such as these should not be viewed as a replacement for a well-trained collection specialist. Rather, these tools should be used to assist the specialist in avoiding the more mundane aspects of correcting and enhancing link collections. This should leave the specialist free to spend more time identifying and cataloging information from new sources.

FUTURE DEVELOPMENT
OF INTERNET SERIALS DIRECTORIES

The Directory of Computing Science Journals represents an interesting prototype in the development of serials directories on the Internet. It seems clear that publishers of academic journals will increasingly provide Internet access to on-line information about them, even if the journal articles themselves are not available on-line. There is no apparent abatement in independent projects to develop Internet-accessible free bibliographic databases in a variety of useful formats. Prediction of increased Internet access to document delivery services and integrated access to library holdings information also seems a safe bet. These trends should make it increasingly likely that Internet serials directories can become a valuable information resource for users looking for information about academic serials.

One important issue for further research concerns the integration of access to proprietary literature databases into Internet serials directories. These databases are of course valuable sources of professionally-maintained citation data for serials. However, the licensing provisions limiting the use of such databases on networks make integration with Internet serials directories problematic. On the other hand, there may be good reason to question the future viability of commercial bibliographic databases if the same information is freely available from publishers and other sources on the Internet.

Another important question is the relationship between Internet serials directories and conventional serials cataloging following MARC conventions. The integration of Internet-based serials into conventional MARC cataloging has been an important topic in recent serials cataloging work.[7] But the model presented by the Directory of Computing Science Journals represents an entirely different kind of serials catalog, one in which the hypertext and world-wide networking capabilities of the Web play a fundamental role. If this model is of value, how can/should it be integrated with more conventional approaches?

REFERENCES

1. Robert D. Cameron. To link or to copy?–Four principles for materials acquisition in Internet electronic libraries. Technical Report TR 94-08, School of Computing Science, Simon Fraser University, December 1994. On-line paper available at http://elib.cs.sfu.ca/project/papers/.

2. David M. Jones. Hypertext bibliography project. Web page at URL http://theory.lcs.mit.edu/dmjones/hbp/.

3. Anthony M. Cummings, Marcia L. White, William B. Bowen, Laura O. Lazarus, and Richard H. Ekman. *University Libraries and Scholarly Communication: A Study Prepared for the Andrew W. Mellon Foundation.* Association of Research Libraries, November 1992. Available at URL http://www.lib.virginia.edu/mellon/mellon.html.

4. Tim Berners-Lee. Universal Resource Identifiers in WWW: A unifying syntax for the expression of names and addresses of objects on the network as used in the World Wide Web. RFC 1630, Internet Engineering Task Force, June 1994. Available at URL http://www.w3.org/hypertext/WWW/Addressing/URL/Overview.html.

5. Roy T. Fielding. Maintaining distributed hypertext infostructures: Welcome to MOMspider's web. In *First International Conference on the World-Wide Web–Proceedings*, Geneva, May 1994. On-line paper and software distribution available at http://www.ics.uci.edu/WebSoft/MOMspider/.

6. Mark S. Ackerman and Roy T. Fielding. Collection maintenance in the digital library. In *Digital Libraries '95–The Second Annual Conference on the Theory and Practice of Digital Libraries*, Austin, Texas, June 1995. On-line paper available at http: //csdl.tamu.edu/DL95/papers/ackerman/ackerman.html.

7. Bill Anderson and Les Hawkins. Development of CONSER cataloging policies for remote access computer file serials. *The Public-Access Computer Systems Review*, 7(1):6-25, 1996. On-line article available at http://info.lib.uh.edu/pr/v7/n1/ande7n1.html.

Index

AACR2 (*Anglo-American Cataloging Rules* 2nd. ed.,), 92,93,99
Abstracting services, 62,198
Academic Press, 29
ACQNET, 144,178,186
Acquisition librarians, involvement in technical services, 205-206
Acquisitions
  automation of, 204
  of e-journals, 92
  World Wide Web home pages for, 178-179
AcqWeb, 178,186
Administrative Notes, 36-37
Adobe, 22-23,29
ALCTS Network News, 144
Algonquin College, 6
Aliteracy, 44
American Association for the Advancement of Science, 27,91,100
American Astrophysical Society, 22
American Library Association, 6
  Government Printing Office and, 34,35
  World Wide Web home page, 183, 186
American Library Association Guide to Cooperative Collection Development, 70,72-73
American Physical Society, 27-28
America Online, 10,42,190
Anglo-American Cataloging Rules (AACR2), 2nd. ed., 92,93,99
Archie, 202
Archives, electronic, 199-200,201
  Los Alamos e-print, 24
  of newspapers, 13,14,15-17

ARPA, digital library grants, 207
Arpanet, 91
Association of College and Research Libraries (ACRL), 92-93
Association of Computing Machinery, 199
Association of Research Libraries (ARL), 197
  directory of electronic journals, 199
  training programs, total quality management approach of, 203
  World Wide Web home page, 183, 186
Astrophysical Journal Letters, 22-23
AT&T Bell Laboratories, 26-27
Author publishing, 61

Bath University, 167
BBS programs, 10,16
Behavioral and Social Sciences Librarianship, 6
being digital (Negroponte), 196
Benedict, Thomas, 39
BIBCO, 110
Bibliographic control, of e-journals, 89,90,99
BibTeX format, 215
Birminghman and Loughborough Electronic Network Development (BLEND), 20
Bodleian Library, World Wide Web home page, 182,186
Books, impact of
  electronic-formatted information on, 44,48-49

   223

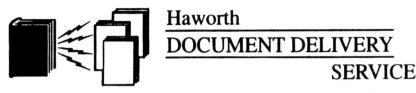

Haworth
DOCUMENT DELIVERY
SERVICE

This valuable service provides a single-article order form for any article from a Haworth journal.

- *Time Saving:* No running around from library to library to find a specific article.
- *Cost Effective:* All costs are kept down to a minimum.
- *Fast Delivery:* Choose from several options, including same-day FAX.
- *No Copyright Hassles:* You will be supplied by the original publisher.
- *Easy Payment:* Choose from several easy payment methods.

Open Accounts Welcome for ...
- Library Interlibrary Loan Departments
- Library Network/Consortia Wishing to Provide Single-Article Services
- Indexing/Abstracting Services with Single Article Provision Services
- Document Provision Brokers and Freelance Information Service Providers

---

MAIL or *FAX* THIS ENTIRE ORDER FORM TO:

Haworth Document Delivery Service
The Haworth Press, Inc.
10 Alice Street
Binghamton, NY 13904-1580

or FAX: 1-800-895-0582
or CALL: 1-800-342-9678
9am-5pm EST

PLEASE SEND ME PHOTOCOPIES OF THE FOLLOWING SINGLE ARTICLES:
1) Journal Title: _____
 Vol/Issue/Year: _____Starting & Ending Pages: _____
 Article Title: _____

2) Journal Title: _____
 Vol/Issue/Year: _____Starting & Ending Pages: _____
 Article Title: _____

3) Journal Title: _____
 Vol/Issue/Year: _____Starting & Ending Pages: _____
 Article Title: _____

4) Journal Title: _____
 Vol/Issue/Year: _____Starting & Ending Pages: _____
 Article Title: _____

(See other side for Costs and Payment Information)

COSTS: Please figure your cost to order quality copies of an article.

1. Set-up charge per article: $8.00
   ($8.00 × number of separate articles) _____
2. Photocopying charge for each article:
   1-10 pages: $1.00 _____

   11-19 pages: $3.00 _____

   20-29 pages: $5.00 _____

   30+ pages: $2.00/10 pages _____
3. Flexicover (optional): $2.00/article _____
4. Postage & Handling: US: $1.00 for the first article/
   $.50 each additional article _____

   Federal Express: $25.00 _____

   Outside US: $2.00 for first article/
   $.50 each additional article _____
5. Same-day FAX service: $.35 per page _____

GRAND TOTAL: _____

METHOD OF PAYMENT: (please check one)

❑ Check enclosed ❑ Please ship and bill. PO # _____
(sorry we can ship and bill to bookstores only! All others must pre-pay)

❑ Charge to my credit card: ❑ Visa; ❑ MasterCard; ❑ Discover;
❑ American Express;

Account Number:_____ Expiration date:_____

Signature: ✗_____

Name: _____ Institution: _____

Address: _____

_____

City: _____ State:_____ Zip:_____

Phone Number: _____ FAX Number: _____

MAIL or *FAX* THIS ENTIRE ORDER FORM TO:

Haworth Document Delivery Service	**or FAX:** 1-800-895-0582
The Haworth Press, Inc.	**or CALL:** 1-800-342-9678
10 Alice Street	9am-5pm EST)
Binghamton, NY 13904-1580	